FIGHT FOR SURVIVAL

FIGHT FOR SURVIVAL

UNDERMINING PSYCHOLOGICAL WARFARE

Jamie Cannon

Copyright © 2019 by Jamie Cannon.

All rights reserved. No part of this book may be used or reproduced in any manner whatsoever without written permission except in the case of brief quotations embodied in critical articles and reviews.

To that girl who was free.

Table of Contents

PREFACE xi

CHAPTER 1 13

Mental Torture

CHAPTER 2 17

History of Psychological Warfare

CHAPTER 3 33

Symptoms of Psychological Warfare

CHAPTER 4 56

The Impact of Religious Organizations on Psychological Warfare

CHAPTER 5 67

Psychological Manipulation in the Legal System

CHAPTER 6 76

What Causes Psychological Warfare?

CHAPTER 7 86

Emotional Intelligence and Psychological Manipulation

CHAPTER 8 91

Will Therapy Work?

CHAPTER 9 100

Skills to Cope with Psychological Warfare

CHAPTER 10 137

The Role of Support Systems

CHAPTER 11 145

Prevention

CHAPTER 12 153

Closure

Appendix A: Case Illustrations 155

References 193

PREFACE

This book is an in-depth exploration of the meaning of psychological warfare (manipulation) and the skills that can be used to survive it. Subject matter is focused primarily on chronic exposure to psychological warfare/manipulation. All case illustrations included in this book are fictional and presented for the purpose of illuminating the insidious nature of chronic psychological manipulation. Unless otherwise noted, the theories and presentation of ideas in this book are the opinion of the author only. Anyone who is aware of reportable abuse of any kind must follow all applicable law and regulations regarding report of this abuse. This book is in no way intended to diagnose, treat, or cure any kind of medical or mental health condition. If anyone is experiencing a medical or mental health emergency, they are urged to contact 911 and follow up with local resources available to them.

CHAPTER 1

Mental Torture

"Do you remember that friend of yours who watched you spank Maggie in that movie theater?" Amber feels the churn in her stomach at his words. "I know how worried you were about it that night." She knows what he is hinting at, in the middle of his tirade about her poor parenting. She can vividly recall the evening it happened, an innocent enough family outing at a local movie theater. Maggie, their 3-year-old, was in the midst of an epic meltdown complete with screaming and waving her chubby little arms around. She was probably tired, or maybe overwhelmed by the animated film. Kevin sat back in his seat with his arms crossed behind his head, calmly watching the movie and seemingly unaffected by Maggie's behaviors. Amber knew it would fall to her to take care of Maggie, so she quickly picked her up and carried her out of the theater and near the restrooms by the front entrance. She offered a small snack secreted away in her pocket in a zip lock, and when this did nothing to lessen the

tantrum she tried singing softly. Maggie was having none of it, screaming louder and trying to kick the wall. Eventually, Amber gave in and spanked Maggie. It seemed to do the trick, and Maggie started to hiccup as her screaming stopped. Amber scooped her up and nuzzled her head, walking back into the theater. She and Kevin were able to finish the movie and soon packed up all their belongings to head to the car. On the way out the door, they passed a group of colleagues of Amber, one of whom was a fellow hairdresser. Amber had noticed one of them on the phone by the restroom when she left the theater with Maggie. Amber was not close to them but waved and smiled as she walked by. Outside, as they were loading Maggie into her car seat, Amber asked Kevin if he thought her colleague had watched the scene with Maggie and the resultant spanking near the restroom. Kevin reassured her that no one had noticed and that even if they had, there was nothing abnormal about their family interactions. Amber sighed and climbed into the van, aware that she was also tired from their long day.

Abuse has many forms. It crosses all ethnicities and socioeconomic lines. It is not a respecter of persons, and there are no concrete methods of identifying to whom abuse will occur. Some abuse is overt and can be seen. Other abuse lies hidden under the surface, waiting to spring out and sink its fangs unknowingly into its victims. The damage from the latter kind of abuse comes in the aftermath of cat-and-mouse games, the veiled threats, and the destruction that is leveled at peoples' lives.

War can be overt, with bloodshed, structured military formations, and weapons of mass destruction. It can involve public and classified meetings of strategy, with attempts to decide what outcomes are worth the cost. This kind of warfare is known to not only result in death and ruin, but research has also started highlighting the link between exposure to ongoing battle conditions and Post Traumatic Stress Disorder (PTSD Treatment for Veterans, 2016). For many people who have been exposed to either active fighting or the constant expectation of military attack of some kind, ongoing issues with mental health can be common. However, others have come to recognize there is an altogether different kind of war that may be less well known but equally insidious and deadly.

Psychological warfare is the opposite of overt, and it is a common tactic used in attempts to control or dominate others. It is invasive, destructive, and seeks to terrorize the very aspects that make up a person's core. The use of this kind of warfare has only one objective in mind – to seek and to annihilate. There is no middle ground, and there is certainly no retreat. To fall victim to psychological warfare can completely demoralize a person and cause them to lose all belief in themselves and hope in their future. Simply put, this type of warfare is mental torture.

CHAPTER 2

History of Psychological Warfare

From a strictly military perspective, psychological warfare is often referred to as the use of propaganda in addition to psychological operations to control and/or shape the thoughts, emotions, and behaviors of others. The use of this tactic has one purpose – to break the enemy, rendering him unable or unwilling to further fight. If used successfully, it can result in complete avoidance of a battle.

From a historical perspective, psychological warfare has been used for centuries. Battle legends have employed this technique in multiple ways throughout the annals of history. Think of Cyrus the Great, who became a leader of what would commonly be known as the Persian Empire, and his quest to conquer Babylon. Through good timing (namely, showing up right when the city's inhabitants were growing disillusioned with their leader) and the subtle spread of propaganda throughout the city, he was able to turn the city against its leadership. His victory came in the form of gaining the newly sworn allegiance of an entire kingdom and their allied armies, with minimal actual fighting. Alexander the Great used his cunning streak to leave behind loyal troops in vanquished cities, with the goal of making friends with the conquered and pushing their assimilation. Troops eventually married locals and started families, further assuring loyalty to Alexander's cause and culture.

Adolf Hitler is one of the most notorious examples of psychological warfare that has been continuously studied and explored. Much research into his personality points to his extreme feelings of inferiority and frustrated interactions with a reportedly tyrannical father during childhood. These factors appeared to combine as an adult to produce excessive needs to exert dominance over others, a severely impaired sense of self-worth, arrogance, impaired empathy, and grandiosity. Hitler was observed to focus his use of psychological warfare primarily on the Jewish race, with an end goal of absolute destruction (Macias, 2016). He commonly espoused a belief that he was validated morally and ethically to execute what has been termed an attempted genocide of the Jewish race, and Hitler used many methods of known propaganda in addition to emotional, financial, and other techniques of control to subjugate the Jewish people. Although his profile could be deemed as a classic one when studying the common elements of psychological warfare, it tends to be more of an overt example.

Another well-known example of use of psychological manipulation was Genghis Khan (leader of Mongols in 13th century B.C). One of the most effective psychological weapons utilized by this leader comprised of threatening total annihilation of settlements unless they first pledged support and tribute to the Khan (Chan, 2007). When enemies refused to comply with these directives, the Khan would intentionally slaughter their population save a few individuals who would be used as witnesses to future settlements of the devastation likely to occur if they refused to swear loyalty to his cause.

Genghis Khan was a master at using threats of destruction and creation of paranoia in forcing civilizations to admit defeat before waging a physical battle (New World Encyclopedia).

Napoleon Bonaparte has been lauded as a military genius. In addition to his military endeavors, he was also a master at presenting a certain image to others. In a time where no mass media existed, Bonaparte was able to carefully represent himself in visual and recorded portrayals to support his desired persona. He commissioned artists to visually represent him according to how he wanted to be portrayed, including such small nuances as portraits not representing the eyeglasses he commonly wore for reading. Some completed paintings of Napoleon even retold history differently than it occurred, with an exaggeration of his deeds as opposed to accurate depiction of the events at hand. Additionally, he controlled the outflow of print and shut down multiple newspapers that had been operating prior to his climb to power (Scanlon, 2014). The importance of presenting a certain image to others cannot be underscored in the era of Napoleon. Any type of weakness or vulnerability would likely have undermined his authority, leading to a potential failure in a military sense as well as a loss of power. Because Napoleon was an intelligent public figure, he deeply understood the necessity of presenting himself in the most positive light to the world in order to retain power as long as possible. His tendency to rewrite the history of the battles that took place combined with his manipulation of printed materials distributed to the "right" people helped cement the peoples' belief that he could lead them to victory. Napoleon also exhibited grandiosity in his personality, often with a seemingly insatiable drive to present himself as an infallible hero (Zamoyski, 2019). There were also many traits Napoleon exhibited that illustrate the potentially positive aspects of psychological manipulation; for instance, his tendency to personally visit the soldiers before important battles, and his recognition of battle accomplishments by his soldiers cemented the solidarity of his armies (Blaufarb, 2012).

Another resounding example in history of the use of psychological warfare was Joseph Stalin. He was notoriously charming when the need arose, exhibiting exceptional skills with people and an innate charisma. Stalin was able to gain trust from others on an intimate level, despite his behaviors that clearly exhibited a belief that people were to be used and discarded when no longer useful to his outcomes. Stalin was brilliant at understanding and using the motivating factors to others' behaviors – often as a tool to gain more power and reach his objectives for his country. Through his use of manipulation and inherent awareness of others' driving emotions and thoughts, Stalin was able to produce almost complete reversals of fortune in World War II. He charmed others easily, provided them with small victories to gain their trust, and used their gratitude toward him to gain what he really wanted. On the surface, Stalin was able to connect with others and appeared deeply interested in their desires; however, history demonstrates that these behaviors were simply a study of character in order to determine how he could use others' desires to gain what he wanted. Although Stalin demonstrated a keen ability to understand others' emotions, he also exhibited consistent disregard of these emotions. He was unfailingly disconnected to other people, unaffected by personal relationships, and demonstrated no remorse for his destruction of others (Rees, https://www.historynet.com/stalin-the-puppetmaster.htm). There were also many associates who were helpful to Stalin's overall goals who exhibited similar characteristics. A notorious example can be found in the following quote about the behaviors exhibited by Stalin's hangman Genrikh Yagoda:

"But his police functions inspire horror. He speaks softly to you as he calls black white and white black, and his honest eyes look at you with amazement if you begin to doubt his word." (Rayfield, 2007).

Psychological warfare can extend far beyond the battlefield. From a clinical standpoint, psychological warfare (also referred to as psychological manipulation) involves manipulation and tactics designed to induce fear in order to gain control of others. It takes aim at our vulnerabilities and desires, using these as a means of achieving objectives. Highlighting fear, humiliation, agony, loneliness, and other painful emotions is one of the top tools used in this type of warfare. From a clinical perspective, this type of warfare has at its base an insatiable desire for power, regardless of the impact of one's actions on others. It seeks to alter the thoughts and behaviors of others through deceptive and abusive techniques.

Psychological warfare has a unique place in our evolving mental health history. Often referred to as psychological manipulation, it remains deadly in its aim to exert power over others through total destruction. In order to accurately understand psychological manipulation, it must be examined in the context of the development of personality. Personality is notoriously challenging to define, and identification of the "abnormal" aspects of personality has undergone an extensive process since the early days of mental health and awareness of mental disorders. As far back as the 18th century, personality was characterized by 4 main temperaments – phlegmatic, sanguine, melancholic, and choleric - all based on the 4 humors of Hippocrates (Crocq, 2013). Through decades of research, theories, and study, personality disorders have been further defined and likely will remain fluid in nature. Personality plays an essential role in the use of chronic psychological manipulation, necessitating a discussion of some of the potential features that may contribute to personality disordered presentations. Included below are some frequent indicators that can be observed when discussing personality characteristics that may fall outside of the "norm:"

- Excessive drive for power and control, failure to conform to known standards of behaviors, lack of empathy and remorse, exploitation of interpersonal relationships for personal gain, dishonesty, manipulation, lack of guilt over behaviors that are harmful to others, focus on revenge-oriented behaviors, persistent anger emotions and/or mood, impulsivity, engagement in high risk taking behaviors with minimal forethought to potential consequences, and irresponsible behaviors.
- Persistent distrust of others and their intentions, even when no rational for distrust exists. Consistent interpretation of others' motives as being malicious, assuming ominous meanings are behind everyday interactions or events, and hesitancy to engage in close relationships due to unwarranted fears that these will be used against them.
- Eccentricity in behaviors, odd and unusual thought processes, unusual beliefs viewed by others as bizarre,

little emotional responsiveness to positive or negative situations, avoidance of social/interpersonal interactions, suspiciousness of others, and impaired empathy and intimacy in relationships.

- Feelings of indifference to others, social isolation, indifference to positive or negative interactions with others, impaired enjoyment of social and interpersonal relationships, and preoccupation with fantasy or introspection.
- Unstable self-image, instability in future goals, impaired ability to recognize the needs and feelings of others, hypersensitivity to interpersonal interactions, difficulties maintaining intimate relationships, preoccupation with real or perceived abandonment, frequent mood changes with easily aroused emotions, intense fear of rejection, depressed mood, suicidal ideation and preoccupation with suicidal themes, impulsivity, engagement in high risk taking behaviors without thought to potential consequences, and persistent anger and irritability in mood patterns.

- Constant need for reassurance and approval from others, inappropriately seductive behaviors, discomfort with not being the center of attention, use of physical attributes and appearance for attention seeking purposes, easily guided and influenced by others, and irrational belief that relationships are more intimate than they are in reality.
- Impaired self-esteem, maladaptive social behaviors, excessive feelings of inadequacy and shame, hesitancy towards any risk taking, preoccupation with perceived rejection or slights from others, impaired desire to initiate intimate relationships out of fear of rejection, avoidance of social activities or relationships, diminished capacity to experience positive feelings, and intense anxiousness.
- Inflated and variable self-esteem, sense of entitlement, constant seeking of appreciation from others, tendency to engage in relationships for purposes of getting needs met in a superficial manner, impairment in empathy skills, attention seeking behaviors, and grandiosity.

- Pervasive psychological dependence on others, pessimistic, fear of rejection and hypersensitivity to criticism, fear of separation, difficulty making decisions without the approval of others, difficulty expressing disagreement with others, feeling helpless when alone, and unrealistic preoccupation with fear of being left to fend for themselves without support from others.
- Sense of self derived from work, constricted expression of emotions, rigid standards of behavior, impairment in empathy, rigidity leading to difficulties maintaining intimate relationships, insistence on everything being perfect, struggles when asked to change ideas or opinions, and perseveration on behaviors despite repeated failures (Diagnostic and statistical manual of mental disorders, 2013).

It is common for certain individuals to possess several characteristics of different personality disorders without meeting the full criteria for one specified disorder, especially in the context of trauma (with an emphasis on childhood trauma). Personality disorders and psychological warfare are not mutually exclusive, and there are several variables that can be found to be correlated in both. For the purpose of this book, personality disorders will not be further explored other than to note that some symptomology of certain personality disordered characteristics can also be found in individuals who engage in chronic use of psychological manipulation.

Many professionals also view psychological manipulation as part of a domestic violence cycle, as opposed to a stand-alone issue. While there has been extensive research, both cross-sectional and longitudinal, on the dynamics of domestic violence, this book will not delve into the unique characteristics of those dynamics. It is well known that chronic psychological manipulation is typically an important factor/aspect in domestic violence, but the power of this technique in gaining control over others warrants that it is also examined separately from domestic abuse.

Research results are clear that the impact of abuse (whether it is physical, sexual, or psychological) is long lasting and invasive. It can influence brain development, self-efficacy, and personal resiliency. As the focus of this book is on psychological manipulation and abuse, it is essential to differentiate a strictly military perspective of psychological warfare from a more clinical viewpoint.

History proves that in general, psychological warfare can be an incredibly useful tool, for both positive and negative outcomes. The majority of examples of these techniques in history tend to be sensationalized due to their negative characteristics, and reality has exposed many uses of chronic psychological manipulation that seem to walk a thin line related to producing positive outcomes. For instance, modern day political advertising on television is a prime example of the use of psychological warfare to demoralize and discredit opponents. On a much smaller scale, psychological manipulation has been used to influence victories over others through behaviors such as an opposing sports team defacing the team mascot of their opponent in order to decrease their focus on the game at hand. Although it primarily operates from a seemingly malicious standpoint, psychological warfare has also accomplished some valuable outcomes. It can be used in situations as innocuous as an expert working to "convince" or influence others to alter poor habits, make positive life changes, etc. "For the greater good" is a commonly recognized ethical term that has been used throughout history to justify the use of these manipulative techniques over time. A very stark military example is the use of atomic warfare during World War II; this method was used by the United States to inflict terror and fear on Japan regarding America's "potential" for further destruction. While hundreds of thousands were killed by the actual bombs, the use of atomic warfare had a far greater impact through psychological manipulation (or intimidation). One of the most apparent gains with the use of this type of warfare is the ability to win battles with minimal bloodshed; in a military sense, this is rationalized through its ability to shorten wars and provide the most success for the smallest sacrifice. Some experts utilize modern psychological manipulation techniques to fight global terrorism, and there have been endless debates on whether this is an ethical way to gain information and reduce violence. For those who have been on the outside of psychological warfare, it is likely much easier to praise its benefits. For individuals who have been subjected to its methods of terror, it is almost impossible to objectively identify any worthwhile profits from its use throughout history.

CHAPTER 3

Symptoms of Psychological Warfare

Psychological warfare is difficult to define due to its complex nature. There is no common symptom list, but there are many similarities in the way this weapon is used to gain power and control over others. This book will seek to explore the different manifestations of symptomology that occur in individuals who employ psychological warfare, with a focus on understanding its very unique aspects.

Emotional Experts: Through training and a natural understanding of human thoughts and feelings, many people find they achieve unbelievable results when wielding the tool of psychological manipulation. In order to be an expert in this type of weaponry, it is necessary to possess an innate awareness of what makes others tick. The driving forces behind human behaviors are thoughts and emotions. If the goal is to control someone else, accurately assessing which of their emotions propels them into certain actions is key to this overall mission. Psychological abusers are adept at understanding what emotions others experience that can be used against them. While many people are driven by pride, fear can actually be a much more motivating emotion. Accordingly, the chilling weaponry of psychological manipulation takes shape – instead of launching missiles made of steel, these individuals use your deepest fear to control your every move. This kind of warfare is sinister and impossible to defend against in conventional ways. Everyone knows you cannot fight what you cannot see.

<u>Skilled Communicators:</u> Individuals who are master manipulators have honed communication skills. They are able to communicate with a wide array of individuals and systems, and they often come across as an expert in many of these systems. These individuals demonstrate charismatic

communication skills and are able to easily entertain others in superficial ways.

<u>Taking Advantage of Intimacy:</u> Defining psychological warfare and delving into its historical background almost makes it seem less personal, when in reality the use of this tactic is arguably an extremely intimate cruelty. Without a close understanding of others' insecurities, motivations, and inspirations, it would be impossible to psychologically manipulate them for personal gain. Therefore, it is essential that an effective psychological abuser is deeply connected to their victim. Because of these dynamics, many psychological manipulators end up being family members, previous or current intimate partners, and friends. This is one of the reasons that victims of psychological manipulation find trusting others to be extremely challenging and why they guard so carefully against appearing to have any vulnerabilities.

<u>Creation of Paranoia:</u> The far-reaching effects of falling victim to psychological manipulation often change lives and can alter the character of those who have been exposed. Since the end aim of psychological

abusers is to exert power over others (and thereby humiliate and destroy them), victims of this abuse often find themselves getting used to constantly looking over their shoulders or waiting for everything to come crashing down. This constant state of being hyperalert and fearful usually extends far beyond the immediate abusive situation – sometimes lasting for years after they have escaped and are living in a safe environment. In turn, this unrelenting paranoia can cause disruptions in healthy relationships and create a cycle of defeat that exacerbates mental health challenges on all levels. Individuals experiencing these symptoms will usually see underlying motives in everyone's behaviors (even when none exist), believe that all people are out to get them, and experience astronomical guilt and self-doubt. Triggers to these thought patterns can be as minor as reading unfamiliar news stories, hearing harmless words that remind them of hidden fears, or returning to a room, location, etc. in which the individual previously experienced the onset of paranoid thoughts. The majority of these individuals will report their thoughts never turn off and cycle through their heads, similar to circling birds of prey.

Subtle Attacks: The purpose of a subtle attack is typically to destabilize victims, thereby reducing their ability to defend themselves. Subtle attacks often leave intended victims wondering whether they were intentionally provoked or if they are imagining the occurrence, and these attacks commonly use sensitive or very personal information to uncover the insecurities of the victim. Subtle attacks often promote themes of degradation of victims.

Blame Projection: Chronic psychological abusers often project blame for their own behaviors onto their victims. This can take the form of scapegoating victims, and it often occurs in very subtle ways, so others do not become aware of the tactic being used. This technique includes blaming the victim's behaviors or choices for the manipulation that abusers are employing against them. Abusers can also blame their victim for the consequences to their own choices and behaviors, with an ultimate goal of portraying themselves in a more positive light. This, in turn, can lead to disrupted relationships between victims and others – including helping professionals. Blame projection can also incorporate accusing victims of malintent or wrongdoing in order to cause defensive behaviors in victims, while abusers are able to mask their own manipulation tactics.

<u>Establishment of Anxiety:</u> Many times, people who have been chronically exposed to psychological manipulation tactics develop anxiety that is so profound it can be debilitating. The paranoia that comes with being constantly hunted by someone who used to be the other half of an intimate or meaningful relationship typically makes it difficult to connect with others in the future. There are deep correlations between anxiety and paranoid thought processes, to the point where alternate realities created by these anxiety-driven thoughts can become very real in one's mind. While those "on the outside" may be able to logically understand that these fears and anxieties are not reality-based, the person experiencing them can become enslaved to them. In efforts to help, loved ones often attempt to rationalize that these worries are not realistic. While this can be immediately reassuring to people experiencing this level of anxiety, the effect is usually short lived. Anxiety stemming from

chronic psychological manipulation is often pervasive and feels almost inescapable to the person experiencing it. It is this author's belief that these levels of anxiety long term likely have significant impacts on physical and mental health; while research has proven that trauma changes brain structure, it would be interesting to conduct similar studies related to chronic anxiety resulting from psychological manipulation. It can also be argued that chronic exposure to these types of conditions is almost synonymous with the experience of chronic trauma.

<u>Excessive Guilt and Fear:</u> As identified earlier, self-doubt and guilt go hand in hand with experiencing chronic psychological manipulation. The more successful an abuser is at finding the right buttons to push, the more likely it is their victim will start second guessing their own actions. This tends to run the gauntlet from reliving seemingly innocent conversations with others to reviving every past mistake and bad choice, with the intense fear that these will be one's undoing eventually. A stark example of this comes from a fictional case illustration of Jenny, a middle aged female who was psychologically abused by a past boyfriend.

Once out of the situation, she continued to find herself caught up in a litany of her past mistakes, stemming as far back as a young child. While no connection between those experiences and her current choices existed, Jenny found it impossible to stop thinking about and imagining the potential life shattering consequences if all her past "sins" were to be exposed. In response, she engaged in a chronic game of cat-and-mouse with an invisible predator – constantly switching careers, relationships, and environments whenever she felt her past was about to catch up with her. Ironically, in this situation she was in fact her own worst enemy; in reality, she had multiple opportunities to create a new, peaceful life, but she had cast these aside out of fear of exposure from a deeply buried and forgotten past. Had she been able to learn the art of letting go and walked out of these terrors, she would have experienced the freedom she was searching for all along. One of the most undeserved wrongs that occurs when exposed to chronic psychological manipulation is the tendency for its victims to ruin their chances of peace and happiness over fear-based reactions to situations that likely will never happen. Additionally, psychological abusers are typically experts at inducing shame and guilt into others. The more intimately acquainted they are with their victims, the easier it will be to instill shameful emotions and chronic guilt in them. These individuals often focus on their victims' failings with the intent of continually reminding them the reasons why they should feel guilty. They can also, at times, exhibit false concern: using warnings or reported "worry" about the victim to undermine their decisions and confidence. Keeping someone in a constant state of guilt, fear, and shame can be a powerful tool to control their behaviors and use them as a means to an end.

<u>Gaslighting:</u> a way of manipulating someone else into questioning their own reality and sanity. This includes telling lies that are outright, blatant, and so unbelievable it is almost laughable. Gaslighters are able to deny, deny, deny – their own actions, situations, etc., even when there is solid proof they occurred. This technique typically involves actions that do not match up with words, making specific alliances with others to turn them against people, hiding information from victims, attempting to change victims from who they are, and using

whatever is held dear to others as ammunition for harm. People engaging in this type of behavior are masters of turning you against someone you once trusted and depended on. They are also experts at finding "followers" who will believe them no matter what and stand with them in any situation. Typically, gaslighters have a large following of people who think they are trustworthy, reliable, and all around a "good person." This manipulative technique requires getting everyone to believe they are the only ones who know the truth and have all the correct information – a type of moral expert - which makes others turn to them for answers and start to mistrust known sources of information (i.e., family members, close friends, media sources, etc.). Gaslighters are experts at telling outlandish tales with a small nugget of truth buried in them somewhere, which increases their own credibility and creates further self-doubt in others. They also usually start out with small manipulations, in a sense testing the waters to see what they can get away with. They typically feign innocence when confronted about these techniques, exhibiting a form of self-righteousness that they have done nothing (nor would they ever do anything) to feel ashamed about. This is a protective measure because it effectively convinces others that gas lighters would never "intentionally" cause harm to others, in addition to it causes others to further question their own perceptions. Gaslighting is a perfect tactic to use in intimate relationships because the stage is already set for a trust dynamic, and use of this technique can make the victim dependent on their abuser for longer periods of time. Interestingly, the term "gaslighting" comes from a play (called Gaslight) in which a man turns down the gas lights in his home and uses manipulation tactics to convince his wife she is imagining the change (Gaslight. Patrick Hamilton. 1938).

<u>General Manipulation:</u> ways of controlling others which are indirect and underhanded. Manipulation tactics range from outright dishonesty to manipulation of facts and use of internal and external circumstances to further personal power and control. Manipulators are constantly placing themselves in the judge's seat, criticizing others and placing blame onto everyone else for any adverse situation (especially those of their own making). Manipulation often comes in the form of the silent treatment,

withholding attention or goods/favors until they get what they want, adopting a victim stance, interacting with others with hidden agendas, and lack of empathy/regard for others' emotions. Many individuals who manipulate others exhibit a common symptom of "sticking to their story" regardless of extenuating circumstances. They are very careful to never break from the character they have created, even when this is based on lies and all evidence conflicts with it. Chronic manipulators need others to believe in their story in order to gain power and control over them. Additionally, it is common with manipulation that these individuals will make assumptions about others' intentions, beliefs, or motives, and act according to those assumptions – even when they are told this is untrue or inaccurate. This type of manipulation is typically utilized as a form of justification for the abuser's feelings or behaviors. Many times, chronic psychological abusers will even offer apologies to others; however, these are often couched in subtle blame toward their victims as opposed to a genuine apology for wrongdoing. Chronic use of manipulation is always about power and control, and people who utilize this tactic regularly will become skilled at recognizing opportunities to take advantage of others.

Upstaging: tendency to distract from manipulative behaviors by focusing others' attention on the abuser's pain of some kind – whether this is physical, emotional, or psychological pain. This can be commonly seen in abusers' attempts to gain what they want from others through influencing their victims to feel sorry for them, or overly focused on the pain or negative circumstances they report to be experiencing. Chronic manipulators also use their supposed negative or painful experiences as a way to trap victims into being perceived as not giving them the help/assistance they "need."

Financial Control: attempts to limit one's access to, control of, or engagement with financial resources and assets. At times this takes the form of concealing financial information from others, such as financial decisions that were made without consulting relevant people and would likely result in conflict or disagreement of some kind. Financial abuse can include restricting someone's direct access to money, refusing to discuss mutual financial situations, insistence on handling all mutual financial matters, refusing to allow victims to work and/or earn their own income, sabotaging potential or current opportunities, restricting access to joint bank accounts, hiding financial assets, spending to the point of incurring financial debt on joint accounts, intentionally hurting others' credit scores, and refusing to contribute income to joint expenses. Financial control can be more overt (direct threats and intimidation to prevent victims from working, accessing finances, etc.) or more subtle (overspending on gifts to a loved one when finances are tight, "forgetting" to pay a bill, etc.).

<u>Sexual Control:</u> manipulation of others, or use of control tactics, to gratify one's own sexual desires. These behaviors are often observed in situations of domestic violence and can include overt sexual coercion and force in addition to more subtle attempts to manipulate others into performing certain sexual acts. This area often includes control of others' physical appearance, which at times can take the form of manipulating intimate partners into dressing or presenting themselves a certain way because it is

attractive to the manipulator. Alternatively, it can be a method of controlling physical appearance based on feelings of jealousy. Sexual manipulators often have an array of stances available to support their behaviors, ranging from use of a victim stance to rationalization for forcing certain fantasies onto others. Since manipulators are used to having things their way, sexual control typically disregards partners' desires, likes, and preferences and is focused only on getting their sexual wants met. The use of guilt and shame are powerful tools in the game of sexual manipulation and enable abusers to keep their behaviors secret. Many sexual manipulators will coerce partners into sexual acts they are uncomfortable with and later use these as a threat of exposure to others. Additionally, sexual manipulators at times will convince partners that demonstrating "love" can only be done through meeting their sexual desires. If victims are reluctant to do so, refuse to do so, or do not engage at the desired level during these acts, manipulators will often use this as "evidence" that their love and devotion is not reciprocal. This sets victims up for a further cycle of power and control in other areas as well.

<u>Victim Stance:</u> psychological abusers feel extremely comfortable as victims. In fact, many of them thrive on showcasing why they feel victimized. "Healthy" individuals are able to work through setbacks, hurts, and negative life occurrences without becoming bonded to these experiences. In contradiction, the victim stance encompasses individuals who consistently attribute negative experiences to being victimized or taken advantage of in some way by others and are unable to move past these experiences. In combination with use of psychological warfare, a victim stance can become a powerful tool. In many ways, a chronic victim stance partners well with psychological manipulation because people functioning from this perspective consider themselves morally right at all times. Additionally, they often believe they have minimal to no responsibility for their actions, are entitled to others' sympathy and attempts to take care of them, and exhibit a strong tendency to blame others for their misfortunes or negative experiences. Psychological abusers often find intense pleasure in receiving sympathy from others, and this stance can help justify their actions toward their victims. If they can convince

others how wronged they have been, it furthers their case of taking no accountability for their own actions toward those who have wronged them. Many psychological manipulators spend inordinate amounts of time and energy "proving" why they are a victim, which often includes rehearsing the wrongs they perceive to have been done to them to whomever will purchase a ticket to the show. They also are adept at reminding others of the myriad of ways they have been hurt, harmed, and all around destroyed by their victims' actions. This sets up psychological abusers perfectly – it gives them an outlet to take their anger out on their own victims, provides justification for their calculating actions, and offers multiple opportunities to perform for their "followers." While there are certainly individuals who are NOT psychological manipulators and experience periods of victim stance in their thinking, this type of perspective seems to pair smoothly with those who engage in psychological warfare.

Emotional Control: as outlined earlier in this book, psychological warfare is bred on understanding and abusing others' emotions. Emotional control runs the gamut from withholding affection when wants are not being met to using emotions as a blunt force weapon to inflict damage in an intimate way. Emotional control typically revolves around an abuser's two favorite weapons – fear and anger; however, it can also include a range of other emotions (humiliation, embarrassment, etc.). Guilt can be a powerful tool to control others, especially when wielded by a psychological abuser. These individuals are masters at continually reminding their victims of previous failures, misappropriating accountability, and covertly influencing others' behavioral choices through the use of scapegoat techniques. Statements like "this would not have happened if you had just agreed to do what I wanted to in the first place" often echo through the empty halls of these relationships, giving birth to inner torment that can drive behaviors in the future. Psychological abusers use emotional control to point out the faults of others in an effort to convince them they are unworthy (of love, attention, better opportunities, etc.). Threats of harm to loved ones are also a form of emotional abuse, as are attempts to isolate victims from support systems. While individuals who are masters at psychological warfare often appear empathetic on the surface, typically this is just a side effect of their intense energy directed at using others' emotions to exert control.

Smear Campaigns: when psychological abusers are unable to control their victims, they often resort to use of smear campaigns as an alternate method of destruction. These typically include attempts to paint the victim in an unfavorable light and convince others to view the abuser as a martyr, or the "wronged one." Smear campaigns are primarily utilized in these situations as methods of destroying a victim's reputation, thereby giving more power and control to the abuser.

Religious Control: while it is undeniable that spirituality is a protective factor across multiple dimensions, psychological warfare unfortunately finds an easy power outlet through traditional religion. Many traditional churches, and even well-meaning religious people, become ignorantly caught up in the cycle of psychological warfare. Manipulators often find a sense of belonging in the church, where use of their skills can help elevate them to leadership positions and feed their need for self-importance. Religious control can include overt techniques to direct the type and amount of "approved" religious activities in addition to more subtle manipulation of the church system to further ingrain an imbalance of power. Individuals who twist religious beliefs and teachings, sharing context that only supports their desires, can wield immense power in these settings and convince their victims of a sound rationale behind their behaviors. The relationship between psychological warfare and the traditional institution of religion will be further explored in later chapters.

<u>Intellectual Bullying:</u> psychological manipulators have a soft spot for showing off their intelligence. Most of them work very hard to convince others they are experts in every sense of the word – and that they will always have the right answer, even when this answer seemingly contradicts reality. If someone practicing psychological warfare tells you the earth is square, no amount of scientific evidence can convince them otherwise. In fact, many of these individuals will use an overwhelming amount of facts and statistics about things that others may know little about in an effort to impress. The

motive behind this type of control is that it provides the upper hand and places them in more of an "expert" position, which furthers a sense of superiority and gives them opportunity to promote their own agenda. Along with presenting themselves as the authority in just about any subject, psychological manipulators also use intellectual bullying to belittle others. Constant harsh judgment of others' actions (even harmless and well-intentioned behaviors) and fostering an impression that there is something inherently wrong with others, no matter how hard they try, is a common tool for these individuals. The majority of the time these judgments take the form of anger at others for not doing things the way they want them done.

<u>Boundary Violations:</u> chronic psychological manipulators are experts at testing the limits and continually pushing them to see when they will break. In these situations, a boundary is viewed as a fluid thing, easily changed, and flexible according to the abuser's needs. Psychological warfare often pushes others' boundaries in multiple ways, such as the following: urgency to respond or make decisions immediately

without forethought, not accepting "no" as an answer and continually looking for "yes" instead, demanding rational for hearing "no" and subsequently arguing with that rational, lack of respect for privacy and space, using coercion or fear to push a boundary and obtain wants, continued revisiting of a situation until achieving what is desired, sneaky behaviors behind the scenes, promoting the belief that you do not have the right to set boundaries, and using others to leverage the desired change in boundaries. Continued boundary violations are common in chronic psychological warfare situations and serve the purpose of wearing down the victim in order to achieve what is desired.

Overall, the varying symptoms of psychological manipulation can range from overt to extremely subtle, making it difficult to recognize these behaviors. When attempting to explore whether a given situation involves psychological warfare, it is recommended to look for an overall pattern of behaviors as opposed to a specific symptom checklist. Some of the manifestations of psychological manipulation can be easily overlooked when examined in the complex nature of human interaction; it is more accurate to look for the general pattern of behaviors that are present in these cases. Most individuals who use psychological warfare do so over an extended period of time, in order to have the necessary periods of trial and error and build the trust needed to be successful in these endeavors. This is another supporting reason why the use of psychological warfare occurs most often within the context of close relationships as opposed to an acquaintance level. The base outcome that underlies all other symptoms in psychological manipulation is an insatiable need for power and control over others.

CHAPTER 4

The Impact of Religious Organizations on Psychological Warfare

As touched on earlier, spirituality has been identified in multiple research outcomes as a protective factor for mental health and well-being. The impact that spirituality has on overcoming tragedy, successfully navigating life's obstacles, and developing a healthy sense of self complete with positive coping skills cannot be denied. Unfortunately, while personal spirituality is indeed a protective factor for victims of psychological warfare, in some cases the traditional institute of religion can be a devastating collaborator for a psychological manipulator. In religious settings that promote superficial charm and "blameless" behaviors and neglect to place an emphasis on the motivation or intentions behind the behaviors (as opposed to what it looks like on the surface), manipulation can run rampant.

Traditional religious settings, at times, can over-emphasize integration and encourage individuals to either abolish, or keep secret, any behaviors that fall outside of "the norm." Psychological manipulators can thrive in punitive environments focused on fault-finding, and many times traditional religious settings can become solely focused on punishment for misbehaviors. Many religious environments also fail to delve into the intentions and motivating factors behind individuals' behaviors, instead centering on how well individuals fit into the framework of their religious expectations. This can set up an environment in which a manipulation to "appear" to fit in becomes the sole effort. For some manipulators, genuine change is not likely to occur – but appearing to change on the surface is a skill they have mastered. This constellation of issues can fit in very well in a religious atmosphere that measures mainly outward behaviors and the "appearance" of doing the right thing. These types of environments may often result in some individuals gaining immense power through manipulation while others become increasingly diminished and experience an urge to hide their imperfections. Additionally, the air of secrecy that can be encouraged by these settings also places victims of psychological abuse at immense risk of having no one to turn to for assistance. If a victim observes their manipulator being lauded as a leader in religious (or "moral") settings while at the same time experiencing psychological distress at the hands of this person, it will further cement the imbalance of power in their relationship. This dynamic can also encourage the victim to experience increasingly impaired self-worth and support their belief in the gaslighting techniques being used by their abuser.

Religious staff, professionals, and clergy often lack the training and reps (real life practice and familiarity) necessary to spot manipulative tactics and address these in a safe, effective way. Despite this, when individuals being victimized are involved in a traditional religious setting, this is typically the first help that may be offered to them. While good intentions may initiate the process of intervention in these situations, these "helping individuals" often find themselves caught in a vice instead of truly improving the situation. Maintenance of a positive reputation and being viewed as morally superior is incredibly important to psychological manipulators – so the stakes are very high when it comes to playing their game. It happens often that well-meaning religious helpers can become hurt, manipulated, and used when they opt to engage in this sport. This kind of help can also place victims at colossal risk, as they typically lose their entire known support system when fighting back against psychological warfare. Additionally, the religious help that is so easy to manipulate can be used as valuable ammunition by the abuser to cause further harm to victims of psychological abuse. Well meaning, but misplaced, help can lead to devastating effects in the long term.

If you are a victim of psychological manipulation, there are important factors to think about when looking at whether to become involved with a religious support system for purposes of intervention and assistance. The most important piece is safety. It is essential to determine whether you are absolutely certain what you share will be kept confidential. In many cases, although clergy themselves are bound by a certain code of ethics and protected under privileged communication statutes (Cassidy, 2003), there are numerous other church staff who are not. Furthermore, if a victim is communicating with only an ordained minister, that person falls under the definition of "privileged communication" in only some states in America – not all. Every country has different regulations regarding the communication that occurs between a "counselee" and their clergy (Radel, Robert, and Labbe, 2015). It is vital for personal safety reasons that each victim research whether the person they are considering seeking advice from fits the necessary role in addition to ensuring they fully understand the laws pertaining to confidentiality issues in the location where they live. Even if the person being sought for advice/guidance does fit this role and does fall under the legal definition of privileged communication, confidentiality can still be a murky subject. Additionally, regardless of the pertinent laws and regulations, there is no guarantee that the religious staff/minister/person will maintain confidentiality. In the cases of couples who have previously sought couples "counseling" from a religious staff/minister/clergy/etc., these roles can be even further blurred if one person of the couple were to seek assistance from the same staff/person related to these issues. Victims can place themselves at immense safety risk in these situations, and a little research can go a long way in determining the level of safety present in communicating these issues to specific religious persons.

Again, while spirituality has been an effective tool in creating support systems and empowering individuals to overcome obstacles, that does not equate to a mentality that all religious environments and settings are a "safe haven" to address these issues by any means. While this is likely a controversial perspective, it reflects the promotion of safety first in all situations, with a focus on completion of necessary research to determine what type of assistance may be the best fit for each victim.

In addition to exploring the impact that religious environments can have on helping victims of psychological abuse, it is also vital to delve into how abusers can take advantage of this structure and setting. As mentioned earlier in this chapter, individuals who have honed manipulation skills often thrive in traditional religious environments. This is due to many factors, but one of the most prominent ones is when an emphasis is placed on one's superficial presentation as opposed to one's intentions. While there are countless examples of traditional religious leaders, clergy, and other staff who manifest fruit according to their belief system, there are many instances in which religious affiliated persons place too much importance on a flawless appearance and not enough importance on motivations and intentions. When leaders in a religious setting ignore the need to examine others' motives and instead focus primarily on their superficial willingness to conform, they set themselves up as easy targets for manipulation as well as allow manipulators to take advantage of this setting to further harm others.

An example of the vulnerability of religious settings to manipulation is found in Betty[1], whose husband was known widely in her church as an alcoholic. Betty spent much of her energy talking about her efforts to rescue her husband from himself, convince him to come to church, and consistently presented to others as a "good" woman just trying to make it through the incredible

---

[1] Fictional representation for purposes of clarification and understanding

burdens she was given to bear. Betty was so ingrained into the church culture that she was asked to serve as a chairperson for a committee on mentoring new members – specifically to use her incredible life experience as a lesson to new believers in earning salvation through self-effort. Betty found it extremely useful to be able to use her long-suffering situation with her husband as an example of why new members should expect life to be difficult at times and to point out the need for perseverance. Betty was so widely revered as a staple in her church, and an unofficial expert on determination of will, that church members were significantly shocked when it came to light that she was not in fact married and had no husband. Following this revelation (made by a neighbor who happened to attend the same church and was surprised to hear Betty's good deeds mentioned in the morning sermon), church members were in disbelief at the betrayal. The incident caused an extensive rift in the church body itself, long after Betty disappeared (which occurred after her immediate attempts to smooth over the revelation failed). The far-reaching impacts could be seen in the new atmosphere of mistrust, fear, and doubt that was manifested in the church body following Betty's disappearance. The reality is that too many individuals were more than willing to judge Betty's outward presentation as holy without examining true intentions. Betty (and the church's) emphasis on appearance and surface conformation provided the perfect atmosphere for her behaviors. Additionally, this situation was based in realistic facts that with just a small amount of checking into would have been quickly discovered.

This is one situation of many that occur in religious settings, and similar situations are often more covert and difficult to decipher what is true and what is not. This incident can easily be picked apart and examined by applying the common symptoms of psychological manipulation described in an earlier chapter. Betty's ability to present as a moral expert with all the answers, her victim stance behaviors and thought processes, her manipulation of others' emotions to use as ammunition for promoting herself, and her gaslighting techniques are all clearly visible in hindsight. Unfortunately, in this situation and many similar ones, hindsight is too late, and many people are injured superficially (and on deeper levels) when these behaviors occur. Additionally, by the time these types of situations come to light, psychological abusers may even have been advanced to leadership positions in the religious setting, placing the organization as a whole at immense risk as well.

While it is impossible to create any environment free of manipulation, traditional religious settings can increase awareness of these issues and the proclivity of individuals to utilize these environments to promote themselves through their psychological manipulation. By providing didactic training to all staff, increasing resources available as references to these issues, and promoting a greater awareness of how manipulation can manifest in these settings, religious organizations could impact positive change in their environment. It is important to emphasize that this training can, and should be, provided by experts outside of the traditional religious field as well as experts within the field. Clinical, legal, and forensic resources could be utilized in these settings to better educate and train religious professionals/staff in order to reduce the manipulation of power and control that can take advantage of and flourish in these environments. There are times when these environments tend to be more closed systems, and increasing their open nature and flexibility is essential to reducing the instances of manipulation that can occur behind closed doors. Because of the power to effect change that religious settings have, it is vital to victim welfare that these environments are aware of psychological manipulation, able to recognize it, and can offer truly helpful interventions to reduce its occurrence.

CHAPTER 5

Psychological Manipulation in the Legal System

The legal system also plays an extremely important role when it comes to chronic psychological manipulation. Unfortunately, it seems to be largely ineffective in its current status in recognizing and dealing with ongoing psychological manipulation and abuse. Legal representatives and personnel often lack the expertise to identify when this is occurring (or alternatively may choose not to employ their expertise effectively) and have not received relevant training to these issues. Individuals utilizing this kind of manipulation are often able to run circles around "experts" in legal settings - they focus on appearing morally correct on the surface, are skilled at utilizing the victim stance role to affect the emotions of others, and typically have amassed large "followings" to evidence support of their statements of grandeur. This type of behavior can come across as very showy in many legal settings but is not a genuine presentation of facts. In some ways, the dog that barks the loudest is the one who often gets noticed first.

Psychological manipulators can regularly use legal environments as an opportunity to practice and perfect their skills, often with the unwitting aid of the legal system. Because the nature of chronic psychological abuse is difficult to concretely define, it can be challenging in a legal sense to establish meaningful parameters around it. This has been apparent in some of the struggles lawmakers have had when trying to broaden the definition of domestic violence to encompass more than physical and/or sexual abuse. Recent administration changes have now identified domestic violence as felony or misdemeanor crimes of violence (justice.gov/ovw/domestic-violence), whereas prior definitions included emotional abuse, manipulation, and coercion in the legal definition of domestic violence. It is unclear whether these changes were in response to funding issues, different administrative focuses, based on research outcomes, or a response to the difficulties in legally proving behaviors such as manipulation and emotional abuse. Domestic violence is a separate issue from the focus of this book, although there are obvious correlations between psychological manipulation and domestic violence.

It is fundamentally complex to define, recognize, and intervene in cases of chronic psychological manipulation. This difficulty is likely the main precipitating factor to the challenging work of the legal system in reducing these tactics, as broader legal definitions open the system up to more room for abuse and error. Additionally, some legal "experts" employ the use of psychological manipulation as an end to their own means. This makes it even less likely for legal environments to invest resources and energy into stopping the use of this tactic in their own settings.

In reality, and within the parameters of the current legal system in the United States, much of the recognition and intervention of psychological manipulation utilized in this environment comes down to an individual awareness, training, and intuition of each legal role and/or representative. Legal representatives who possess integrity and do not use this tactic for their own gain stand to learn the most from being educated on the symptoms of psychological manipulation. Education and training on these tactics, as well as real life familiarity with these issues during the training process, can be the most effective tools in increasing awareness of these issues in the legal system. Because individual experiences, knowledge, and character will always impact the way that professionals recognize and interact in interpersonal settings, it is essential that legal representatives are trained in the concepts of transference and counter-transference as defined below:

<u>Transference:</u> redirection of feelings and desires, especially those unconscious ones from childhood experiences, to a new object (person).

<u>Counter-transference:</u> in clinical terms, the therapist's total reaction to a client.

Transference and counter-transference historically have been clinical terms, used in therapy settings (Freud, 1912). However, they relate to legal representatives just as importantly. Unfortunately, although legal agents absolutely relate in certain ways to other individuals based on their own experiences and unconscious beliefs about them, they do not receive enough training on understanding the emotional dynamics inherent in their professional relationships and interactions. Unconscious emotions and thoughts can, and do, impact the feelings that legal representatives have toward others, which in turn impacts the decisions that are made in legal settings (Gordon, nassaubar.org/articles/transference-and-countertransference-a-psychoanalytic-perspective-on-the-attorney-client-relationship/). These impacts range from an individual level to a macrosystem level (such as policy changes). When transference and counter-transference are not recognized or understood, it can lead to a disaster in these environments. Psychological manipulators are extremely talented at sensing the transference and counter-transference issues that occur around them, often on a subconscious level, and they utilize this knowledge to mold situations according to their desires.

In order to decrease the manipulation that can occur in the legal system, especially in cases that depend largely on the personal judgment of legal agents, it is vital that legal professionals receive more training on transference and counter-transference issues. They must be able to objectively evaluate professional relationships and situations and disengage from the transference/counter-transference dynamics impacting their decisions. This is the first step in "tearing down the veil" that often separates legal agents from the reality of their professional interactions. Once legal professionals become adept at recognizing the transference and counter-transference issues that could impact their decisions and behaviors, it is necessary for them to be able to step back and use this knowledge to increase objective decision making. This increased awareness and training, coupled with real-life reps and experience, can greatly reduce the use of chronic psychological manipulation in legal settings. Because of the power dynamics and control that is exerted when psychological abuse is allowed to occur unchecked in legal settings, victims can find themselves further oppressed in these environments. It is critical for victim empowerment and protection that legal representatives are able to recognize these tactics and intervene when they are used.

Another tool that can be utilized by legal professionals in relation to psychological manipulation is to recognize the hallmark symptoms of this abuse and take patterns of behavior into consideration when working with others, making legal decisions, etc. History is one of the best measures of future behaviors, and in the case of chronic psychological manipulators it is crucial that professionals recognize the underlying behavioral patterns that indicate their history of use of manipulative tactics. These individuals may frequently change their environment, but their behavioral patterns will usually remain the same. There are times when this is extremely difficult to recognize, as chronic psychological manipulators tend to keep one particular victim "in their sights" as long as they are able to, prior to moving on to another victim. Additionally, they will often utilize victim stance thinking as evidence that their inappropriate behaviors are justified toward that victim (i.e. they do not act this way toward others currently in their life, their behaviors are a result of being hurt by that person, etc.). This is due to the abuser receiving "nourishment" from their abilities to continue psychological abuse of that one victim; as long as they are allowed (and in many cases empowered) to continue abusive behaviors toward that individual, they will often not seek out other victims. When a victim is no longer available to them for patterns of abuse, psychological manipulators can often be observed at that time to move on to other victims.

As pertaining to the legal environment, it is essential that legal professionals are able to differentiate between someone who is genuinely "a changed person" and someone who is just continuing to get their needs met because of ongoing psychological abuse of one victim. Of the hallmark symptoms that make up these behavioral patterns, one of the easiest to recognize is whether individuals are able to take true accountability for behaviors. The majority of psychological manipulators may appear to take accountability on the surface, but when explored in depth it will become evident very quickly that their belief is these behaviors are a result of being wronged by someone or some situation. These beliefs are utilized as supporting evidence as to why it is acceptable for them to continue to engage in abusive patterns toward certain people. Most chronic psychological manipulators are monogamous when it comes to their victims;

as long as they are able to exert power and control over that individual, they most often continue to engage in these dynamics until they are stopped.

In conclusion, psychological manipulators can (and do) abuse the legal system to further their games of power and control over victims. Without oversight, training, and experience, legal professionals will continue to fall prey to this and further perpetuate abuse that is traumatizing to its victims. It is critical that any professional in the legal system is aware of these behavioral patterns, knows how to recognize them, and is mindful of the subjective role their own experiences and emotions play in their professional judgments and interactions with psychological manipulators.

CHAPTER 6

What Causes Psychological Warfare?

As with common medical and mental health challenges, many people want to explore the etiology of psychological warfare. More commonly referred to as "what makes them tick," studying the commonalities in backgrounds for individuals who psychologically abuse others is an important factor in determining etiology. While psychological manipulation can be found as a part of several personality disorder symptoms (Diagnostic and statistical manual of mental disorders, 2013), this book does not seek to create any new clinical definitions of established disorders. Rather, it is an exploration of the technique itself and ways to undermine its effectiveness. That being said, in order to fully understand the use of psychological manipulation and increase ability to recognize it, it is important to explore potential etiology behind these behaviors.

There is no common, known, and traceable background in individuals who employ psychological manipulation consistently, although there are some similarities that need to be discussed. Furthermore, there is also no common average use of this technique in individuals employing it. Some people use it consistently to the point of it becoming a hallmark of their personality, while others use it sparingly and only in certain situations. As identified earlier in this book, there are some potentially positive outcomes associated with use of psychological manipulation. As a clarification, etiology of this technique here is mainly focused on individuals utilizing it for purposes of power and control personally, as opposed to use of it to produce positive outcomes for the greater good.

Many individuals become psychological abusers from exposure to this as victims in their childhood. In these cases, individuals often learn these techniques from having them employed on themselves as well as unconsciously learning the effectiveness of these tactics through observation and modeling. Modeling is a powerful learning tool, and when children are exposed consistently to psychological abuse from primary caregivers it can shape their personality and interactions with their environment for the rest of their lives. Children reared in environments with psychological abuse as a common theme can learn dysfunctional ways of loving others, receiving love from others, and developing relationships. This can lead to continued dysfunction as an adult and in their own caregiving roles, perpetuating a cycle of manipulation and abuse if interventions are not successfully implemented. It goes without saying that children can also be incredibly resilient and seemingly out of nowhere develop a healthy sense of self and positive ways of interacting with their world despite consistent exposure to abusive situations in childhood.

In individuals who become psychologically abusive and have no known early exposure to this style of interacting with others, acute and chronic trauma exposure can play a role in development of these tendencies. Trauma experiences force individuals at times to develop unhealthy coping mechanisms, and the possibility of learning to use psychological warfare in response to undergoing traumatic events exists. Research is clear that trauma is powerful and can occur at any time in life; development of maladaptive coping skills in response to trauma can have far reaching effects regardless of the age it occurs at. This type of psychological abuser typically stops the use of these tactics once they are removed from the traumatic situation and have stabilized. In situations of chronic trauma, obviously the potential to use psychological abuse as a coping skill escalates.

Some individuals who employ chronic psychological manipulation have been defined as "psychopaths." Psychopathy has been clinically defined as a disorder manifesting the following: behaviors that do not conform to known moral/ethical standards, inability to establish reciprocal intimate and interpersonal relationships, extreme focus on oneself and one's needs/wants at the expense of others, and difficulties learning from experiences or prior behavioral patterns and their consequences. Historically, psychopathy research has indicated that this disorder is related to character and behavior (Hermann, 2017). Research has even found structural differences in the brains of individuals who fit criteria for psychopathy, including impaired connections between areas of the brain responsible for emotions such as empathy, guilt, fear, and anxiety (Motzkin, Newman, Kiehl, & Koenigs, 2011). There have been some studies done that have identified the increased presence of individuals with psychopath labels in certain career paths, further illustrating the ability of individuals possessing these symptoms to appear as high functioning, successful adults. One researcher has conjectured from his work that psychopaths are more often found in careers that involve risk taking (Dutton, 2012).

An important take away from this research is that psychopathy does not appear to prohibit high functioning in individuals across the board, and in fact some individuals who have received this label experience significant success in career outcomes. There are some obvious commonalities between psychopathy and symptoms of chronic psychological manipulation; while this may be one potential causal factor to the chronic use of manipulation, there needs to be further research regarding these propositions to determine true cause and effect. Additionally, there are many individuals who employ chronic psychological manipulation/warfare and do not meet the full criteria to be labeled as psychopaths.

There are certain hallmark features that can commonly be found across psychological abusers. These are further defined below:

<u>Unrealistic expectations of relationships</u>: expectations that relationships will be textbook perfect with no communication issues and no problems.

<u>Hypersensitivity:</u> tendency to overreact and be extremely sensitive to perceived slights from others. Typically includes an over response of retaliation to being hurt or embarrassed.

<u>Distrustful nature:</u> distrusting patterns in all relationships and interactions with others, not just in intimate relationships.

<u>Insecurity:</u> impaired sense of self-worth and insecure about personal abilities.

<u>Entitlement:</u> feeling they have an inherent right to never be hurt or embarrassed and to receive what they want at all times.

<u>Lack of empathy:</u> difficulties putting themselves in the place of others; challenges

when trying to understand others' motives (with a tendency to assign negative intentions where none exist).

Ingratiation: focus on impressing others who are perceived to have power or access to power, with the intent of using their influence for self-serving purposes.

Deferred accountability: tendency to blame others and lack of ownership of one's own feelings, thoughts, and behaviors.

Arrogance: inflated self-esteem and grandiosity, centered on one's worth, abilities, and talents.

Impaired emotions: reduced experience of range of emotions, with use of emotions such as remorse, guilt, etc., only being exhibited for self-serving purposes.

Restricted emotions: tendency to exhibit a short and superficial range of emotion (i.e. angry, sad, or happy, without any other emotions) including anger dysregulation and use of anger to control others.

Grooming behaviors: psychological abusers engage in what is known as grooming, or building connections with others for the intent of gaining their trust – making it easier to manipulate them.

<u>Need for approval:</u> the seeking of others' approval is all encompassing and drives behaviors. This is closely related to an inflated sense of self-worth, as gaining others' approval underscores the individual's grandiosity.

<u>Need for power and control:</u> often tied into impaired self-control, a strong need to advance their own personal gain and desire to feel powerful over others. Feelings of superiority in interpersonal relationships are a common underlying feature.

Just as there are certain features that are common across the spectrum of psychological abusers, there are also characteristics that can be similar among victims of psychological abuse. Because this subject matter pertains to human intricacies and the complex nature of interpersonal interactions, there is no "one size fits all" to be able to predict who may become a victim, or an abuser, in these situations. However, there has been extensive research done related to commonalities experienced, for both victims and abusers, that can help increase awareness of the formation of these issues. Included below are some frequent characteristics that can be found in victims of chronic psychological abuse (Center for Substance Abuse Treatment, 2014):

- Childhood experiences of trauma and manipulation
- Unhealthy desire to please
- Low self-esteem
- Fear of confrontation
- Lack of assertive communication skills
- Emotional dependency on others
- Fear of being alone
- Lack of support system
- Over-internalization of others' opinions

Again, resiliency is extremely difficult to measure – and many individuals who undergo experiences that could potentially contribute to development of psychological manipulation instead become functional adults capable of developing and maintaining healthy relationships. There are no concrete, known factors that will <u>always</u> lead to the development of psychological manipulation/warfare. In some ways, hindsight comes into play again when determining precipitating factors. Recognizing commonalities in individuals who become psychological abusers is more likely to provide a level of comfort and understanding to victims as opposed to offering any methods of predicting and stopping development of these characteristics. However, it is well known that understanding the formulative factors behind a behavior increases the likelihood of being able to develop effective responses to that behavior.

CHAPTER 7

Emotional Intelligence and Psychological Manipulation

Emotional intelligence is one's ability to recognize and understand emotions and utilize this information as a guide for decision making. This skill is a basic skill that chronic psychological manipulators utilize, thus warranting special examination in the context of this book.

Emotional intelligence is fluid and can be improved and developed over time. It is, like any other skill, something that is both impacted by environments and can in turn impact environments and outcomes. In order for an individual to possess effective emotional intelligence, they must be able to recognize emotions in self and others, regulate emotions safely and efficiently, and utilize awareness of emotions to inform decision making processes. Empathy is also an integral aspect of emotional intelligence, and there are two widely recognized types of empathy: affective and cognitive. Affective empathy refers to the ability to experience the emotions that others experience, whereas cognitive empathy is more related to the capacity to understand others' emotions.

While emotional intelligence has been correlated with improved social outcomes, higher overall achievement academically, enhanced well-being, and more positive interpersonal relationships, (Mayer, Roberts, and Barasade, 2008), it can also be utilized as a tool for manipulation. Chronic psychological abusers are typically adept at recognizing the emotions of others and using these to gain power and control over their victims. Interestingly, although these individuals often demonstrate a decreased range of emotions themselves, they are regularly able to identify emotions in others. Many chronic manipulators are able to take advantage of positive emotions in others by pressuring individuals into decision making based on their upbeat feelings in the moment; conversely, they also are able to utilize negative emotional states to play on fear, guilt, shame, etc. As discussed previously, human behaviors are motivated by thoughts and emotions; this uncanny ability to recognize intuitively the emotions of others provides chronic psychological abusers with ammunition to gain control over others' behaviors.

There have been numerous studies conducted to determine whether individuals who employ chronic psychological manipulation also possess emotional intelligence. Psychopathy (consistently antisocial behavior with hallmark features of limited empathy and remorse) has been found to be positively and negatively correlated with emotional intelligence. Research seems to suggest that emotional intelligence can be used in maladaptive ways to impact interpersonal relationships (Nagler, Reiter, Furtner, and Rauthmann, 2014). Individuals who employ chronic psychological manipulation regularly need to be able to manipulate others' emotions in order to be successful in their endeavors. Without the use of some aspects of emotional intelligence, it would be impossible for these individuals to effectively manipulate others. However, research on this topic indicates that these individuals likely do not possess emotional intelligence overall as a personality trait, but rather possess certain aspects of this skill that they use to manipulate others.

Perhaps it is important to differentiate between being able to recognize others' emotions and truly understanding and sharing these emotions. Individuals who chronically manipulate others may be skillful at recognizing and labeling the emotions that others experience, but they likely do not share or understand these emotions. Recognition of emotions in these instances is more likely a means to an end, as opposed to true emotional intelligence. Psychologically abusive individuals are frequently able to adapt to different situations well, which is also a characteristic of emotional intelligence; however, in the context of psychological manipulation, this adaptability is more often a feature that allows these individuals to better manipulate situations because of their ability to "fit in" so easily. An additional hallmark feature of true emotional intelligence is the ability to regulate one's own emotions; chronic psychological manipulators typically do not exhibit emotional control across multiple settings. They tend to exhibit emotional control in situations that support their end goals, but behind closed doors often do not regulate emotions effectively. Additionally, the ability to differentiate between a need and a want can also be an essential piece of emotional intelligence and is characteristically absent in individuals who employ chronic psychological manipulation to control others.

It has been well established that numerous protective factors come as a result of possessing emotional intelligence. This book does not seek to promote a viewpoint that chronic manipulators have developed emotional intelligence; rather, it is important to distinguish that psychological abusers may take advantage of some of the aspects of emotional intelligence in order to promote their own outcomes and to gain control over others.

CHAPTER 8

Will Therapy Work?

The million dollar question with psychological manipulation is how do we stop it from victimizing others? Since it is primarily categorized as a behavioral/mental/personality issue, one of the first interventions that most people turn to is clinical therapy of some kind.

Behavioral health therapy is extremely varied. Not only are there multiple types of therapy that are based in sound research and practice, but there are also varying degrees of practitioner expertise. The mental health field as a whole has struggled to be viewed as a medical science, despite the numerous evidence-based practices that are able to produce long lasting change as a result of behavioral health therapy. Because of the extensive research that has been conducted on mental health therapy, this book will not delve into the specifics of available interventions in a general sense. However, it will seek to address the efficacy of known best practice interventions as related to psychological abuse/manipulation.

Overall, the "prognosis" for individuals who have become adept at chronic use of psychological manipulation in their interactions with others is not good. While early intervention is always a key, individuals who have honed these skills without effective treatment intercession over a long period of time will likely not make significant gains in a therapeutic setting. This is not to say that therapy cannot, or should not, be attempted in these situations. Rather, it is important to think of therapy in these situations as a method of assisting these individuals to decrease the amount of damage they do to others. It is highly unlikely that an individual who has become accustomed to engaging in psychological warfare for years at a time will be able to make use of therapy to the point of stopping these patterns of behavior. However, it is likely that with effective interventions, they can learn to get their needs met with the least amount of harm inflicted on others. An example would be assisting a psychologically manipulative individual to channel their energies into a high-profile career that would require these characteristics in order to be successful. In this case, it could be a realistic expectation that this individual may not develop long lasting and meaningful interpersonal relationships, may jump from job to job, may move often, but could be successful in the overarching career path due to their talent and chronic implementation of psychological warfare techniques. Expecting someone who has honed these skills over a long period of time, and rarely engages in meaningful ways with others, to form healthy interpersonal relationships is setting everyone up for a failure. Additionally, victims already in these relationships can be placed at further risk of harm if false hope is instilled regarding the long-term prognosis for chronic psychological abusers.

One of the most effective mental health "theories" that has been supported with decades of research regarding its ability to produce long lasting change across multiple domains is Cognitive Behavioral Therapy (CBT) (Beck, 2011).The basic premise of this therapy is the connection between thoughts-feelings-behaviors, with an understanding that our behaviors are influenced by our thoughts and perceptions. Employing strategies to identify and overcome maladaptive thought patterns often leads to behavioral change as well. Some of the hallmark components of CBT are listed below:

- Increasing recognition of overall thought patterns, with a focus on which thoughts may be unproductive or unrealistic
- Learning beneficial ways of thinking and behaving
- Understanding the impact of past experiences on current perceptions and behaviors
- Distinguishing between facts and irrational thoughts
- Increasing awareness of our automatic thought processes that impact our behaviors
- Increasing awareness of our learned behaviors that may not be beneficial

It is fairly evident by a brief examination of CBT principles that this type of therapy can likely address multiple areas and issues. Research is very clear that CBT works well for many mental health challenges, including depression, substance abuse/addiction, anxiety, persistent mental illness, impulse control issues, and more (https://www.apa.org/ptsd-guideline/patients-and-families/cognitive-behavioral). There have been studies conducted on the use of CBT in domestic violence, with some efficacy demonstrated. Several of these studies approach violence in the context of domestic abuse as a learned behavior, with the end goal of helping perpetrators learn nonviolent behaviors instead (National Institute of Justice). However, when it comes to the effectiveness of CBT interventions with chronic and persistent psychological abusers, there is little evidence available to indicate a strong and direct correlation between treatment and positive, long term change/outcomes. CBT interventions can help reduce the damage that is done in these situations through increasing awareness of maladaptive thought patterns as well as teaching concrete skills for redirecting and reforming related thought patterns. While this would likely produce at least short-term behavioral changes, in many instances it actually serves to provide more opportunity for these individuals to hone their skills. In some cases, increasing awareness of these interventions can also increase the use of manipulative tactics, in part because CBT employs techniques aimed at better understanding how people think, feel, and behave. As discussed in earlier chapters, understanding what makes others "tick" is one of the basic skill sets of psychological manipulation.

There are many other evidence-based types of mental health therapy, ranging from psychodynamic (talk therapy based on early experiences, bringing to light repressed emotions/experiences, focus on individual's relationship with the external world) (Mecke, 2006) to interventions focused on strength building and motivation to change. Research is extensive on these mental health theories, with positive results being demonstrated in numerous studies for multiple mental health issues. However, when dealing with psychological manipulation, there is no one size fits all model that can predict positive outcomes across the board. Many psychological abusers have been effectively treated by combining an array of therapy techniques, but many others have struggled with worsening of symptoms following treatment interventions. While individual therapy can highlight early experiences that led to formulation of these techniques as well as increase awareness of triggers to the need for power and control, in general, the long-term forecasts for chronic psychological abusers in therapy remains gloomy. This is not to say that interventions should not be attempted; however, there remains a caution that this is done with someone highly trained in treatment of these symptoms in order to avoid creating further opportunities to increase this maladaptive skill set.

It is important that the emphasis of any therapeutic interventions be to reduce the harm inflicted on others through learning new ways to meet wants and needs. Professional expertise is the key in these situations, in order to decrease opportunities for manipulation and enhance safety of all involved to the extent that is possible. Treatment of these issues should be provided by professionals who are aware of the inherent risks, have experience with treating manipulation, and are able to reduce counter-transference (when a professional projects their own emotions onto a client). It is imperative that professionals treating these individuals are able to establish a therapeutic rapport without assisting further manipulation to take place as well as do not use their own pre-formed opinions and life perspectives to impact their work with this population. Additionally, there should be a caution when it comes to administering instruments/assessments to individuals who are skilled at psychological manipulation. These individuals will often be able to manipulate the outcome of these instruments, including assessments that have built in validity measurements to guard against this. Professionals must be able to interpret any assessment/instrument outcomes in the light of the individual's presenting issues, in addition to look at the "whole picture" of presenting issues as opposed to just the manipulator's representation of facts. Anything to the contrary could place victims at further risk through production of invalid results. Additionally, there are some instances in which assessment results are utilized to make clinical and even legal decisions that impact the welfare of the individual in question, as well as others; this further highlights the need for treating professionals to have many reps completed in recognizing and handling these presenting issues prior to working on these cases.

Individuals who are chronic psychological abusers rarely seek therapeutic interventions on their own. Most often, there is a precipitating catalyst that leads them into seeking professional help. At times, this can come in legal form as well as ultimatums from support systems/relationships. Regardless of the reasons that triggered professional assistance, it is extremely important that all involved are aware of the potential risks involved in treating this symptomology. It is equally important that this treatment is done in a very planned and structured manner, to avoid causing further damage to potential victims.

CHAPTER 9

Skills to Cope with Psychological Warfare

The title of this book is intentional. Living with chronic psychological warfare is a fight for survival in ways that are not easily visible. Not being able to see the battle you know is going on around you can be devastating and lead to extreme challenges in learning how to combat it.

To be clear, this book promotes the end goal of survival but recognizes that many individuals are able to conquer these situations and go on to lead lives of quality. However, many instances of exposure to psychological warfare are chronic and not an experience that one can escape or walk away from. Because of the intimate nature that characterizes the use of psychological manipulation, many of these situations take place in family or intimate partner settings. While immediate safety should ALWAYS be at the forefront, some individuals will not have the luxury of ending all contact with their abuser. This book will not go into details regarding mandatory reporting of abuse laws, etc. other than the emphasis that if a situation is dangerous and you have witnessed or experienced reportable abuse, it is necessary to follow the applicable abuse reporting laws. Unfortunately, in the case of psychological abuse it is often extremely difficult to prove it has occurred without exposing oneself to a repeated and well-documented pattern of abuse for extended periods of time, which serves to further re-traumatize victims. Additionally, if the abuse is reported and nothing is done to correct it, or the system is manipulated by the abuser, it creates even more danger and distress for the victim.

Given the unique presentation and nature of psychological manipulation, survival skills to combat these tactics need to be equally distinctive. The majority of psychological warfare cannot be met head on in an offensive battle, due to the very insidious and underground nature of the weapon itself.

Attempting to offensively combat psychological warfare without a well thought out and rehearsed plan of action can lead to a range of outcomes, from complete disaster to an all-around failed mission. If psychological abusers become aware that victims are "on to them," (which in their eyes will lead to less vulnerability on the part of their victims), their game can become increasingly more violent and toxic. It is ideal that victims of psychological abuse separate themselves from the situation and danger whenever possible. However, in reality it can be more effective to view this battle as a marathon as opposed to a sprint, with awareness that there are many situations where victims cannot leave or terminate contact completely with a psychological abuser. In these situations, teaching victims to "out-think" their abusers is the key, with an emphasis on keeping oneself as safe as possible in each unique situation.

Inventory of Vulnerability

Most successful battles begin with a comprehensive, solid battle plan. This is no different in the context of undermining psychological warfare. Victims must develop a plan that encompasses a range of topics and issues; psychological abuse takes on many forms and is extremely complex. Battle plans to address it must also be complex and all-inclusive, leaving no stone unturned. Development of a battle plan in these situations typically feels rehearsed and can be painful in many ways, which will be explained in more detail below. However, it is a necessary step to survival.

Battle plans to undermine psychological warfare need to begin with a review of the victim's areas of weakness. It is essential that victims are excruciatingly honest with themselves about any potential area in which they are more vulnerable to an attack. Common examples of vulnerable areas include the following: an addiction problem, history of trauma, the involvement of children in the situation, risky behaviors, extramarital affairs, and so on. It is recommended for victims to take an inventory of these areas in their lives and increase their own awareness of how someone could use these vulnerabilities against them. There is an old saying that if you know your own buttons, it will be less painful when others push them. This is true in the case of psychological warfare –

knowing your areas of vulnerability gives you time and energy to build up defenses in those areas. If a victim knows they have an addiction problem that could be used against them, immediate treatment for the issue and positive change that can be demonstrated to others is essential. If a victim has made poor choices in relationships, developing new methods of establishing and sustaining healthy relationships is an immediate area to address. Everyone is vulnerable in some way; the difficulty with victims of psychological abuse is the constant use of their vulnerabilities to disgrace, humiliate, and punish them by their abuser. This creates a cycle of shame and can lead to the development of depression, anxiety, and even suicidal behaviors by victims. By taking stock of their vulnerabilities ahead of time and brainstorming the ways they can be used to hurt them, victims will be able to regain some sense of power and a clear direction on what work is needed next. This is often a very painful process and can create feelings of anxiety and paranoia. Realistically, if a victim is chronically exposed to psychological manipulation they cannot escape, it is not far from the truth to be experiencing a sense that someone is out to get them. Using these feelings to increase their own recognition of weak spots in their armor can decrease feelings of paranoia in the long term.

It should be noted that one cannot plan for every potential vulnerability and develop a way to protect against and remediate them. There will be instances where abusers are able to find new or unrecognized areas of weakness and use these to continue manipulative patterns. Victims need to be understanding of the limits they each have and accept they are not all-knowing. Mistakes will happen, they will choose the wrong path at times, and chances are this will be used against them in some way. These issues are part of being a human. Unfortunately for victims of ongoing psychological manipulation, they often do not get the "slack" that others may experience in response to messing up.

No Response is the Best Response

Once victims have a well-rehearsed awareness of the areas they will need to defend against, it will be necessary to identify a plan for defense. The absolute, most important lesson in undermining psychological warfare is to hone the ability to wait for the right moment. Victims of ongoing psychological warfare are constantly being hunted, threatened, and provoked. Learning to have no response to these provocations and attacks until the perfect moment is essential. There is no sense in wasting ammunition by engaging in ground fighting before you are in range to use the big guns. Victims must learn to be silent in response to their abuser when it doesn't count – and in the case of psychological warfare this will be extremely hard for many individuals to determine. For instance, when an individual's character is attacked and they are being humiliated in front of extended family members or acquaintances, it may seem like the perfect moment to launch a defensive measure. However, most character assassinations can be ignored, with the idea that people who matter will not believe them or will directly approach the individual in question to see if they are true. If friends, acquaintances, and family members are easily caught up in the blame game that is spread by abusers, it would be a better expenditure of energy to educate THOSE INDIVIDUALS on the tactics being used as opposed to directly confronting the abuser. Recall the symptoms of a psychological manipulator – a strong victim stance and complete dishonesty (even in blatant situations) are hallmark characteristics. The likelihood of victims changing these characteristics is almost non-existent in cases of chronic manipulation, whereas the chances of opening others' eyes in a non-judgmental or blaming manner to the tactics being used are much higher.

Being silent in response to attack is a very challenging and uncomfortable role for most people. The majority of individuals today, including high profile and everyday people, tend to feel the need to defend immediately and engage in verbal back and forth arguments when they are personally attacked. When victims learn to be initially silent instead, it creates a power differential between them and their abusers. This can often throw their abuser off, prompt them to up the ante in their attacks, or look for new ways to attack. While this seems counterintuitive to the end goal, it is actually the opposite. This puts victims in the driver's seat in a way, because through their silence they will accomplish several things. Primarily, they will not add more ammunition to their abuser's attack by saying unhelpful things in response to strong emotions (anger, fear, embarrassment, etc.). Secondly, they will not engage in uncontrollable and aggressive behaviors focused on demeaning others (unlike their attackers). Lastly, silence allows victims to stop and think about a clear course of action as opposed to making decisions in the heat of the moment, which typically leads to a misstep or missed opportunity of some kind. It is extremely important to clarify that this position does not promote victims "rolling over" and allowing continued abuse. This defensive position is specifically aimed at individuals who have no escape route from chronic psychological manipulation and who need to be able to stay in control of their own reactions in order to make the best offensive moves at the best time. Offensive attacks that are impulsive, not well planned, and undertaken in response to strong emotions often fall flat and are unsuccessful. It is far better, for long term success, that victims adopt a more guarded and cautious method of protecting themselves.

Although it sounds unfair in many ways, victims who are silent and cautious will often find more ammunition of their own to use. In situations where a victim presents as calm and respectful, in response to an abuser's multiple character assassinations and constant blame, they will most likely be viewed as the one who is in control (in addition to making more well thought out decisions). It behooves victims of this abuse to learn to not be as affected while building their own case for solid decision making and ability to control themselves under pressure. Keep in mind that psychological manipulators never have the end goal of collaboration and cooperation; their ultimate goal is always some type of power and control over others. Victims who learn not to be moved by these tactics will regain their own power in some ways, in addition to learning how to formulate more solid defense plans.

Predict the Future

While maintaining personal control and learning how not to respond to attacks is one of the first lines of defense, being able to think in a predictive manner will help victims immensely. There is an intense amount of paranoia and worry that plagues victims of ongoing psychological abuse. They are deeply aware that their every move is being watched, their mistakes can and will be used against them, and their joy of life is being hunted. In situations where everything seems unpredictable and nothing is for sure, these victims must learn how to think one step ahead of their abusers. They must become intimately familiar with the patterns of behavior their abusers exhibit, the triggers to these behaviors, and the typical methods their abusers utilize to attack them. Most psychological manipulators rely on tried and tested tactics that have worked for them multiple times. Victims will need to increase awareness of these and be able to predict which of these techniques their abuser will use in response to which common situations. Victims of chronic psychological warfare tend to adopt a belief pattern that the world is out of control and others are always out to get them. While this is true as related to their abusers, it should not extend to all relationships. Victims can learn to navigate through these abusive environments by recognizing patterns of manipulation that are occurring. As discussed earlier, it is very rare that abusers deviate too far from their known patterns of manipulative techniques that have worked for them so well; victims can learn to recognize these techniques and understand the outcomes abusers have experienced by using them. This will help decrease the fear that victims experience as well as increase their sense of control over what "may" happen to them.

Stop Personalizing Attacks

Another significantly helpful characteristic that will assist victims in undermining psychological warfare is to develop a "thick skin." Separate from learning not to respond to attacks, a thick skin will help victims learn how to stop personalizing these attacks. Psychological abuse can be very damaging, and it is self-protective for victims to learn how to let go of what their abuser says and does towards them. Learning that the abuser's behaviors and words are not really about the victim and are more about the abuser is a useful way to reframe thinking in the midst of attacks. Refusing to own the opinions and feelings of their abuser is also protective for victims, especially those whose abusers utilize the blame game and victim stance repetitively. Victims must learn to take ownership only of their own thoughts and feelings and allow their abusers to think/feel/do whatever they decide to. Coming to terms with their inability to control their abuser can be a powerful means of letting go in addition to the start of being able to undermine the influence their abuser has on their own outcomes.

Know Basic Human Rights

When coping with chronic psychological abuse, it is essential that victims know their basic human rights in order to recognize when these are being violated by their abusers. Victims must be able to recognize the importance of standing up for their own rights, in the safest and most effective way possible. Basic human rights include (but are not limited to) the following: the right to life, liberty, and security of person; the right to not be enslaved; the right to not be subjected to torture or cruel, inhuman, or degrading treatment or punishment; the right to not be subjected to arbitrary interference with privacy, family, home, or correspondence; the right to not have honor or reputation arbitrarily attacked; the right to freedom of thought, conscience, and religion; and the right to freedom of opinion and expression (United Nations, 1948). Only when victims recognize and understand their basic human rights will they be empowered to work towards reducing/stopping violation of these rights by their abusers.

<u>Recognize Triggers</u>

Triggers are any experiences that lead to a reminder of abuse. The classic definition of triggers has become generalized and is a buzzword in society. However, the ability to recognize triggers that exist in patterns of chronic exposure to psychological manipulation can be lifesaving for many victims.

Triggers can come in many forms – they range from visual images to certain smells. Most triggers first occur in the context of the 5 senses, and they immediately invoke visceral reactions in victims. Many triggers with psychological abuse can lead to immediate fearful thoughts about the potential of what could occur; this is a direct relation to the unique type of abuse that victims of psychological abuse suffer from. Because of the importance of recognizing triggers, some common trigger examples are listed below.

- On her drive to work, Aimee noticed a red Nissan pass her that

immediately brought back images of her ex-boyfriend, Rick, pulling over in his car and forcing her out on the side of the road to walk home after an argument. Her hands started to sweat, and she had a difficult time focusing on her driving the rest of the way home.
- During a work meeting, Ted's former colleagues dropped in to say hello. Their presence immediately took him back to the atmosphere of work at that time, which involved a psychologically abusive supervisor. He was unable to remember what these colleagues said or did in the meeting, aside from primary introductions, because of the flashback he experienced during the remainder of their visit.
- Megan was at dinner with her family when she smelled the aroma of meatloaf someone ordered at the next table. The odor prompted her to remember the many times she made this meal for her ex-husband. Because it was one of his favorite meals, this memory was also coupled with recollections of the

hateful things he would say to her that precipitated her making this meal for him. She remembered that although she hated the taste of meatloaf, she often cooked it for him as a way to say she was sorry for not measuring up to what he wanted from her. Megan lost her appetite at dinner because of these memories and was unable to finish her meal. She refused to return to that restaurant several weeks later, when her family said they wanted to dine there, because of the strength of the trigger she now associated with that specific restaurant.

- Alice was reading a good book by her bay window when her phone rang. The caller ID was someone from Idaho. Her hands started shaking and her heartbeat sped up. She felt out of breath and sat staring at the phone. After it went to voice mail, she immediately snapped out of it and realized that the number looked like the one her grandfather had before he passed away. Seeing the Idaho number on her phone reminded her of the nasty voice mails he would leave her after she moved out of the home. She could not shake the memory of the ways he would try to punish her for leaving home, including the attorney calls that started coming from the same area shortly after she left. The phone call ended up being a telemarketer, but Alice was disturbed enough she put her phone on silent and left her book, unable to finish it. Every time she picked it up to continue reading, the memories instantly came back. She finally left the book for good and never finished it.

- George loved Sundays. He loved the feel of his small town as everyone went to church, and he loved that he was able to visit with his neighbors on the walk to church. As he walked to church this Sunday, he felt content and looked forward to the sermon. Once he was seated and the choir started his good feelings vanished. They started with a song that was new to the church but extremely familiar to him – it was the song his mother used to play whenever she was in "that mood." It all came back to him in a second – the things she said, the way she treated him, and how she made him feel about himself. He found himself shaking, on the verge of tears, until the song ended. George was not able to listen to the sermon and couldn't remember anything that was said. On the walk home he was quiet and withdrawn.

- Rosie hates her job. She works in the healthcare field, at a local hospital. She wanted to be a nurse ever since she was young but now wishes she could be anything else. Every morning on her way to the hospital, Rosie feels a growing sense of dread. By the time she checks in for the day, her stomach aches. She has started having headaches almost every day too, even the days she does not work. The worst part is that she cannot trace her feelings to any particular event – she just feels impending doom in her gut. Her therapist has helped her draw the connection between her abusive relationship and a fear that something horrible will happen to her. She understands these fears relate to a sense that she cannot control what happens at work – what she has done in the past or what others may do around her in the future. Anytime someone at work says they need to talk to her, she can feel her heart do flip flops in her chest and has trouble breathing. She is constantly terrified that nothing will turn out well in her job and spends hours paralyzed by these fears. She would give anything to quit immediately and withdraw to some kind of job that is completely different. She is free from the abusive relationship and now just wants to be free from the fear that her world will come crashing down around her.

Although triggers can be instantaneously experienced, the effect of them tends to last for several minutes to several hours. Victims often identify a general sense of unease, paranoia, and increased anxiety following the experiences of triggers; this is the body's method of responding to a perceived threat. In essence, these responses focus the victim's system on "high alert" in order to remain hypervigilant in case of further threats to their safety. While this is understandable from a survival standpoint, when it is chronically experienced it can be exhausting for victims and even contribute to health complications long term due to increased stress on their bodies. It also detracts from current circumstances and experiences because emotions and thoughts become centrally focused; victims often identify decreased memory functions following the experience of these triggers and large amounts of time can pass by with victims unaware of what is happening. The more often triggers are experienced, and the longer the effects of these triggers lasts, the higher the risk that victims will undergo blocks of time in which they are not fully aware of what is going on around them. This is due to the body's tendency to send all cognitive and emotional resources to the area of highest need, which in these situations would be the subconscious threat of danger that the victim is coping with.

It is important for victims to recognize the warning signs of triggers in order to immediately employ known coping skills to reduce the aftereffects of these triggers. Because of the lingering impact they can have on emotions, thoughts, and behaviors, it is crucial that victims learn to recognize the origin of triggers as soon as they occur. It is also protective for victims to gain a general sense of understanding of what type of experiences lead to their triggers, as this can help them avoid them altogether or prepare for the experience of a trigger when these situations cannot be avoided. Being able to avoid and/or manage triggers as they arise can be a valuable tool for victims in coping with chronic psychological abuse.

Reduce Self-Defeat

Negative self-talk can be a symptom that individuals are struggling with personalizing information they receive. Learning to recognize this self-talk, understanding its detrimental effect on oneself, and reframing it by focusing on hopes and goals for the future are important steps to master. Taking things personally can often be related to being overly focused on oneself; in the case of ongoing psychological manipulation, victims often become exceedingly attentive to their own faults and needs. This is likely directly correlated to the onslaught of attacks they are constantly experiencing, but this type of self-focus can be disastrous in these situations. Eventually, when victims are experiencing this negative cycle, they will end up giving their abuser more power and control. In essence, they are taking on their abuser's work for them by beating themselves up internally in response to ongoing assaults. In turn, they set themselves up for failure in nearly every situation due to the internal negative cycle that goes on. This outcome is the one that most abusers will be seeking; if they can convince their victims they are worthless and the abuser is morally correct, they will have a blank check to treat their victims however they desire. Additionally, many abusers seek to produce this outcome because it will increase their chances of getting their victim to do or give them what they want. In light of these potential outcomes, victims MUST learn to reverse their negative self-talk and defeating personal beliefs. Learning healthy self-respect and focusing on one's strengths and successes will empower victims and confound abusers.

Going back to a central theme of this book, developing a "thick skin," in part, is being okay with appearing inferior. Victims should remind themselves that appearances are deceiving and the opinion of individuals who would choose to believe the negative things their attacker says about them are likely not valuable opinions to begin with. This further underscores the importance of educating loved ones, friends, and acquaintances who may fall prey to the manipulation. If a victim can genuinely exhibit non-defensiveness and a lack of regard for the opinion, statements, and thoughts of their abuser, they will be more likely to develop an educated support system that is committed to their wellbeing. If a victim continually becomes agitated and distressed at being colored in a negative light by their abuser, this will only serve to provide their abuser with more power and ammunition and isolate them from potential support systems.

A strengths focused perspective can be a game changer for victims of chronic psychological abuse. Cycles of self-defeat and punishment can become commonplace in these situations; developing an ability and desire to focus on personal strengths can reverse these unhealthy cycles. When victims learn the power they possess to not only recognize their own strengths but also use these to undermine the manipulation that is occurring, they will ultimately be more successful and resilient in the long run.

Prepare for Loss

Development of a thick skin is not just important for interactions with a psychological abuser. Victims of ongoing manipulation will inevitably need to lessen their dependence on other people. There will be loved ones, friends, and/or acquaintances who believe the abuser's tactics and draw away from the victim. This is a very excruciating side effect of being exposed to chronic psychological warfare. Victims must know ahead of time that there will be relationship losses along the way; while they can educate loved ones and friends to a certain degree, at some point those individuals must make their own decisions. This will obviously not always be in the favor of the victim, and when this happens it can create a sense of despair in addition to the grief that will be experienced. It is important for victims not to downplay the loss this entails and to allow themselves to fully experience it. Being aware ahead of time that this will likely occur does not lessen the blow, but does help victims to develop healthy coping skills to manage the associated heartache.

Guard Against Rebound Relationships

Because much chronic psychological manipulation occurs in the context of intimate relationships, many victims of this type of abuse fall into rebound relationships fairly easily. In the framework of this book, a rebound relationship is used to indicate a relationship similar in nature to the chronically abusive relationship an individual victim is experiencing. When victims are in the midst of psychological warfare, they are often more vulnerable to initiating new relationships in general; they are even more susceptible to becoming involved in relationships that take advantage of them. Due to the chronic stressors, paranoia, and anxiety they are experiencing, these victims often fall prey to manipulative relationships, even in the midst of trying to escape them. Relationships that appear to be too good to be true, arise seemingly out of nowhere, and appear to be an answer to all problems, are likely red flags for potential rebound relationships. It is crucial that victims pay close attention to their state of mind and emotional wellbeing prior to beginning new intimate relationships; if any indicators of psychological manipulation are present in these relationships, victims must end them immediately. The unique vulnerability that is created in the environment of chronic psychological manipulation can wreak havoc on future intimate relationships.

Find an Outlet

Another very important tool to undermine the effects of psychological warfare is finding an outlet for victims. When victims are under chronic stress, anxiety, and paranoia that come with this type of manipulation, they can easily isolate and withdraw from others. Many victims no longer have the energy needed to engage in activities they once enjoyed, and these isolative behaviors can further de-stabilize their moods. Finding an outlet that feels comfortable, is safe, and will promote overall wellbeing is essential to victims surviving chronic psychological warfare. Outlets should not include any type of destructive behaviors or habits that could lead to further instability or create weaknesses to be manipulated (think substance use, etc.). An effective outlet can be as simple as taking a walk for 5 minutes a day in a beautiful area, talking to someone who is non-judgmental, drawing/painting, reading for fun…the list of potential natural supports is endless. Victims of chronic psychological manipulation often find their joy in life has been robbed from them. It is very challenging for individuals to constantly be looking over their shoulder, hypervigilant, and aware they cannot make mistakes because they could be used against them; being able to have an outlet for pent up energy and emotions can be vital to victims' welfare. Many victims will want to establish an outlet that is something they can do alone, and although this is difficult for support systems at times, it could be a side effect of their sense of being constantly hunted. For many, being able to do something enjoyable on their own, away from any potentially judging eyes, with no expectations can be a tremendous release. Victims will often feel guilty engaging in any type of activities that are fun, as they have become accustomed to a state of constant mistrust, fear, and anxiety. Likely, victims of ongoing psychological abuse will feel a need to always be on high alert and be working towards "fixing" what is happening to them – this can contribute to their feelings of guilt when they are presented with an opportunity to enjoy something. However, it is important for victims to remind themselves continually that experiencing joy in life can still be accomplished even in the midst of their fight to survive. Below are some concrete ideas on how victims can establish an outlet to promote stability and release:

- Reading for fun
- Exercise/physical activity
- Journaling/writing
- Music
- Taking long drives
- Cooking comfort food
- Traveling
- Reading scripture
- Playing with your children
- Watching an enjoyable movie
- Hiking
- Swimming
- Yardwork/gardening
- Shopping
- Taking a nap
- Taking a bath
- Massage/spa

It is essential that victims do not have the expectation of themselves that during their engagement in enjoyable activities they will be able to "forget" what is happening overall in their lives. The fight to try NOT to think about something typically ends in thinking about it even more. If victims can give themselves permission to think about what is happening while they engage in their desired activity, many times they will find these worries decrease without effort. It is also very important that victims work towards not apologizing for time spent in enjoyable activities. A common theme in individuals experiencing chronic psychological manipulation is a tendency to apologize for the "good" or "fun" things that happen to them. This is a skill that must be mastered by these victims, as it can interfere with the protective factor of finding pleasure in life. Being able to find moments of pleasure can be a survival tool for people to cling to when they are exposed to chronic psychological warfare conditions, and it can provide hope for individuals who otherwise become eaten up by the weight of their experiences.

Spirituality

Although parameters are necessary to ensure safety for victims in traditional religious environments, spirituality is a tremendous coping skill that can be utilized to combat the devastating effects of psychological manipulation. Spirituality provides individuals with meaning, hope for the future, and is often the first step to healing from patterns of chronic abuse. Individuals who possess strong spiritual beliefs and incorporate these into their daily lives have been found to exude more positive life satisfaction (even those individuals who have experienced abusive situations). (Redmond, 2014). Victims who are able to develop resiliency through the use of spiritual coping tools often go on to lead lives beyond the abuse they have suffered at the hands of psychological manipulators. An individual spiritual journey is often the most powerfully transforming coping skill for victims of chronic psychological abuse, and it provides minimal opportunity for traditional religious settings to perpetuate the abuse that has occurred. Additionally, spirituality can often unite victims with common experiences through a faith community; this can be tremendously healing in and of itself. The experience of others, combined with a deep spiritual sense of meaning, can lead to long term healing of wounds and scars.

Guard against Loss of Self

Victims of ongoing psychological manipulation often become one dimensional, focused only on the abuse and exploitation they consistently experience. They can commonly lose interest in work or quit employment altogether, lose important relationships, withdraw from loved ones, stop engaging in enjoyable leisure activities, and forget the unique characteristics that make them who they are. Many individuals in these conditions wake up one day to realize they have actually grown familiar, if not comfortable, with an environment in which they are paranoid and hypervigilant – it has become their "norm." This is, in part, a way for their brain/body to normalize what is going on and increase their ability to survive it. However, in the long term this can spill over into other relationships and create difficulties. Paranoia, worry, and hypervigilance that seep into healthy relationships and everyday experiences can wreak havoc with a victim's internal stability. It can also lead to loss of relationships that are supportive and helpful. Because of these possible consequences, it is important that victims are aware of the capacity for these issues to occur and carefully monitor to reduce this potential. Surviving psychological warfare has much to do with learning to cope with the symptoms that can spill over into other areas of life and trying to negate the effects of these as much as is possible.

In some ways, victims of chronic psychological manipulation exhibit similar characteristics to individuals who are in shock: difficulties experiencing emotions, disconnection from surroundings and events, preoccupation with thoughts and worries, and a sense of numbness. These behaviors and emotions can serve as a protective factor from the intensity and gravity of the situation victims are experiencing. They can also serve a defensive function from loss of hope for the future. If victims were fully aware of the menacing cloud hanging over them at all times, they would likely feel a need to give up. No one wants to work toward a future that feels like impending doom no matter what they do (even if they are perfect in every way, which is humanly impossible). Being aware of this potential can help victims better understand their reactions and feelings at certain times, and it can assist them with guarding against drowning under the weight of what they are experiencing.

Develop a Support System

Individuals experiencing ongoing psychological abuse need to develop a support system to survive. This may be one of the most daunting coping skills, due to many factors. Victims in these situations chronically mistrust others and are paranoid about the intentions of others (for good reason). It is very common for them to assume everyone is out to get them and assign mal intent where none exists. These understandable reactions can create difficulties establishing and maintaining healthy relationships, and they can lead to problem solving issues in existent relationships. Another factor that impacts development of a support system is the abuser's tendency to attack support systems and/or drive wedges between victims and their loved ones/friends/acquaintances. This is a common technique that is used in psychological warfare, and it can eliminate support systems quickly and easily at times. Additionally, many support systems may become exhausted just by watching their loved one go through the effects of ongoing psychological manipulation; this could become wearing on loved ones, friends, and acquaintances fairly quickly and lead to even more difficulties in maintaining support systems.

Because of these unique factors that impact the extended family members and friends of victims, it is important that special attention is paid to educating support systems. This is covered more in depth in a separate chapter; however, the need to establish support systems must be addressed as a separate coping skill in and of itself for survival of ongoing psychological abuse. Victims will need people "in their corner" so to speak, unconditionally and forever. While these people themselves could change over time, it is critical to victim welfare that they are able to establish these connections and maintain them in some way. Support systems will serve many roles for victims, ranging from venting to support in more formalized settings (employment, the legal system, etc.).

It is important to note that due to the distinctive characteristics of psychological warfare, victims should ensure their support system is small but cohesive. They likely will cause more harm than good by establishing an extremely large system that could more easily fall prey to the tactics of their abuser. Victims' "circles of trust" need to be tight knit, comprised of individuals who can withstand the inevitable attacks on their character that will occur, and also be unconditional in their support.

A Special Discussion on Therapy

Behavioral health therapy can be an extremely useful tool in learning to cope with chronic psychological manipulation. Victims are urged to use this whenever possible – with some cautions regarding this service. For behavioral health therapy to be successful, clients must find a therapist who has expertise in their area of presenting issues, is a good fit for them personally, and adheres to ethical codes. Because situations discussed in this book are characterized by intense patterns of manipulation, it is critical that victims of this type of abuse find behavioral health therapists who have experience and reps in this type of work. Therapists are human and can be manipulated, no differently than clergy members, doctors, etc. Victims of ongoing psychological warfare need to develop a therapeutic alliance with someone who is an expert at recognizing manipulative tactics, strictly adheres to confidentiality, and is familiar with coping skills to be utilized to remediate the effects this type of abuse can cause in victims' lives. Without these safeguards in place, therapy could cause more harm than good. If done correctly, therapy can be valuable in treating the mental health issues that can develop and/or increase in response to chronic psychological manipulation. When someone is chronically exposed to these conditions, it can be very common for depression, anxiety, and other mental health issues to arise.

The in-depth exploration of factors that impact victims of chronic psychological manipulation presented in this book can suggest a dark and dreary existence for these individuals. In order to paint an accurate image of the immense weight these individuals are carrying with them every day, it is necessary to explore the depths of what COULD happen under these conditions. This is essential for two main reasons – primarily for victims to see and understand that what they are going through is real, has happened to others, and can be survived. It is also important for others to gain a clearer understanding of the far-reaching effects of being exposed to psychological warfare in chronic conditions. Victims of these conditions can, and often do, not only survive but also find ways to thrive. Personal resilience and available protective factors have a lot to do with this. However, enhancing understanding of these issues through realistic exploration and representation of facts helps to improve the outcomes for victims. This is an overarching goal of this book – to increase the welfare of victims of chronic psychological manipulation.

CHAPTER 10

The Role of Support Systems

For loved ones or friends of victims who may be reading this book, it is essential for their long-term success that you remain supportive and unconditionally accepting of the situation they are in. While it may be exhausting and painful for loved ones to observe the effects this chronic abuse has on the victims, losing pieces of one's support system because of this can be devastating to victims of abuse. As these needs are specific to victims of chronic versus acute psychological abuse, loved ones must be aware that there may not always be an escape available to victims. Although immediate separation from abusive situations is the ideal goal, support systems of victims must be aware that this is not always possible.

There will be times when loved ones are also negatively impacted by the "smear campaigns" that abusers will employ. The motivation behind these attacks is to separate the victim from their support system; an isolated victim will have far fewer resources available to fight back. If support systems can remain united despite the ongoing attacks and hurtful things that will be said about them (and done to them), there is a far greater likelihood that victims will be resilient.

An area that is particularly challenging to support systems of these victims is their sense of powerlessness. Standing by while loved ones are continually attacked, humiliated, abandoned, and shattered is incredibly painful. Loved ones, in many ways, are also victims of the abuse that occurs in these situations. Abuse is centered on power and control, and psychological manipulators thrive on incorporating loved ones into their games. This sends a very effective message that support systems are being punished for caring about the victim. It also helps to drive wedges between the victims and their support systems, which creates chaos and draws attention away from the abuse that is occurring. Loved ones must also bear the burden of not responding to these repeated attacks until the timing is right, because to do so prematurely could further harm the victim. Essentially, psychological warfare creates a system of terror that has far reaching consequences to even those remotely involved.

Below are some skills that can help loved ones of victims navigate situations of chronic psychological manipulation:

<u>Unconditional positive regard:</u> acceptance and support of the victim regardless of what mistakes they have made, what their abuser accuses them of, what they are feeling, etc. Since it can be very tiring to see someone you love become agitated and distressed over the same things repetitively, it will be challenging for support systems to demonstrate unconditional positive regard at times. Often, loved ones feel the need to point out to victims that their reactions are exaggerated, that they should just "let it go," and that they should not allow their abuser to impact their feelings. While this is usually well intentioned in the hopes of helping victims develop a thicker skin, unfortunately it can also serve to isolate and divide. Victims must learn on their own to stop personalizing what their attackers say and do. Loved ones should view their role in this as providing the

"unconditional" part of positive regard. Victims who have been exposed to ongoing psychological abuse will have learned that love is conditional in every sense of the word, but support systems have the potential to help them unlearn this maladaptive pattern of interacting with others through the use of unconditional positive regard.

Trust: support systems must be able to trust what victims tell them. It is vital to the wellbeing of victims that they are believed and do not have to "argue" their point with loved ones. In order to help victims, especially ones who are subject to gaslighting, survive the chronic exposure to abuse they experience, support systems need to be able to agree with them in their experiences. When a support system engages in patterns of disbelief, attempts to debate victims out of their certainties, and plays "devil's advocate," it only serves to further alienate the victim. This type of reaction can also create self-doubt and invalidate the experiences victims are going through. One of the most important factors for support systems to be able to trust victims is their understanding that psychological abusers rarely treat others in the same way they treat their victims. While they may use and manipulate others, and support systems inevitably will be impacted by the abuser, they typically focus the majority of their vindictiveness on one specific victim. Additionally, chronic psychological abusers tend to use other methods of manipulation and harm only for the end goal of devastating, isolating, and destroying their identified victim. These characteristics could lead support systems to doubt the severity of what victims report, making it all the more crucial that they trust victims regarding their unique experiences.

Marathon patience: chronic psychological manipulation is wearing and exhausting to those who are affected by it. Support systems of victims will experience this, both directly from the attacks on themselves, and indirectly through watching their loved one be continually abused. Support systems need to look at these situations as a very long marathon. In situations where there is no escape to the psychological manipulation, victims and their loved ones need to have enough endurance to finish the race. With chronic manipulation, it sets everyone involved up for failure when individuals expect a short resolution to these issues.

<u>Self-Control:</u> just as it is essential for victims of psychological manipulation to possess control of their emotions and behaviors, it is equally important that their loved ones do the same. Although support systems will be attacked in the process of chronic psychological warfare, the more they are able to maintain steady and calm reactions, the more positive the outcomes will be. Support systems that become overly emotional, lash back at abusers in uninhibited ways, and take attacks personally will cause more stress in an already overtaxed situation.

<u>Understanding:</u> for victims of psychological warfare to find a healthy outlet, they will need support systems that are educated and understand the reality of their situation. Many victims feel as if they have to fight their loved ones too, due to their limited awareness of the reality of living under chronic manipulation. When loved ones are ignorant of victims' experiences, thoughts, and the debilitating internal effects that occur with this exposure, they often add more fuel to the fire. Victims of chronically abusive situations will often become anxious, paranoid, and edgy. This can be misinterpreted by support systems and lead

to conflict within the system, drawing more attention away from the situation at hand. For long term success, it is imperative that victims feel their loved ones understand why they think, feel, and act the way they do. This knowledge and understanding will also validate what victims have been experiencing, which can be freeing in and of itself.

<u>Willingness to have fun:</u> while it may sound frivolous, a support system that is willing to focus on enjoyable experiences will greatly improve the morale of victims. Most victims of chronic manipulation expend all of their energy on surviving; they have none left over to enjoy the lighter side of life. Even during instances of engagement in enjoyable activities, victims are often lost in their thought patterns related to their fear of what could happen to them. This can exert a heavy toll on victims and lead to thoughts of despair and lack of hope for the future. At times, these individuals can feel completely unable to cope with the idea that they cannot escape the torture they are routinely exposed to. Having a support system that takes time and resources to engage in pleasurable activities together can be a true lifesaving device for victims. It can infuse them with hope, distract

them from the gloomy present, and help them focus on the positive.

The support systems of victims in general have a heavy burden to bear. In situations of chronic psychological warfare, they often feel they are fighting an unseen enemy with no end in sight. It is vital to the wellbeing of all involved that loved ones are educated, supported, and encouraged to be an active part of this process. Being successful at undermining the effects of psychological warfare is in part dependent on the quality of support available to the victim.

CHAPTER 11

Prevention

As discussed on multiple levels in this book, psychological warfare has many facets and far reaching consequences. The focus on exposure to chronic psychological manipulation is necessary in order to increase awareness for victims and provide solid ways to combat this menace. From a systems perspective, it is important to explore what options (if any) exist to reduce the occurrence of this type of abuse.

In most instances of mental and medical health issues, prevention is the key. The earlier that education and intervention occur, the more resilient individuals tend to be. This is certainly true in the context of chronic psychological abuse and manipulation. Victims who become educated feel they are not isolated in their experiences and learning concrete methods of responding to these experiences will increase their overall resiliency. These individuals will also have a greater likelihood of facing a hopeful future, which in turn can decrease the negative outcomes of mental health challenges in this population. Macrosystems must examine the processes currently in place that may be contributing to the development and use of chronic psychological manipulation, with an increased focus on prevention and early intervention.

Research is clear regarding the correlation between exposure to chronic traumatic conditions and resultant mental and medical health issues. It is this author's opinion that being exposed to chronic psychological warfare conditions is similar to exposure to chronic trauma in multiple ways. Victims can develop many trauma symptoms in addition to some characteristics that are unique to psychological manipulation. Clinical professionals often reference "protective factors" when it comes to determining an individual's resilience, and there has been extensive research done on effective interventions for trauma in order to increase victim resiliency. Some of the most well-known of these protective factors are included below (Brown, 2017):

- Social connections – presence of unconditional loving and caring support systems, characterized by dependable and stable interpersonal relationships
- Responsiveness of systems – the general responsiveness of systems interacting with victims, to their abuse and unique needs as related to their experience of trauma
- Access to needed care – victims' ability to access the necessary levels of care to address and resolve trauma as well as initiate the healing process from trauma
- Economic stability – ability of victims to support themselves economically and provide for basic economic needs, such as housing, medical care, and food
- Spirituality – use of spirituality in the healing process and to develop restorative connections
- Personality – victims' sense of identity, achievement orientation, problem solving capabilities, etc.

play a critical role in trauma resiliency
- Sense of humor – the ability to engage a sense of humor regarding experiences can positively impact the outcome of trauma

These interventions and protective factors should also be examined in cases of exposure to chronic psychological manipulation. Additionally, victims of chronic psychological warfare conditions exhibit a range of other mental health challenges that can, and should, be addressed with early interventions to promote their long-term survival and success.

Being able to access professionals who are aware of the nuances of chronic psychological manipulation and well versed in recognizing these patterns is essential to victim resiliency. Professionals across multiple settings (clinical, medical, legal, religious, etc.) need to be able to master the following skills in order to better assist in the prevention process related to psychological manipulation:

- Recognize patterns of manipulative behaviors (acting differently towards people who are not the

victim, sudden "changes of heart" that are professed to have instigated behavioral changes, superficial charming, exhibiting behaviors that are in contrast to what is being spoken, dishonesty, violation of boundaries, etc.)
- Understand fundamental human rights (being treated with respect, the right to say "no," the right to one's own opinion, etc.)
- View from a distance (find ways to observe potentially abusive individuals across multiple settings rather than just the setting they present to you, be able to recognize patterns of behaviors that occur with their primary victim and do not occur with individuals the abuser perceives as having power to give them what they want)
- Focus on the manipulator through analytical questions (do not allow the potential manipulator to distract and refocus on potential victims, through the use of probing and exploratory questions and observations)

- Set clear boundaries (do not allow potential manipulators to cross boundaries and set clear, firm expectations from the beginning – boundary violations and "pushing the boundaries" are common symptoms in psychological manipulation)
- Intervene when possible (use available resources to intervene on the behalf of victims, fearlessly, and with the end goal of reducing psychological manipulation)
- Listen to intuition (pay attention to internal signals that make you feel uncomfortable in the presence of a potential manipulator, cause you to feel exhausted when interacting with or thinking about interacting with potential manipulators, or create situations where you attempt to avoid interacting with potential manipulators, etc.)
- Guard against unearned trust (check out all the facts, listen to all perspectives, and utilize your observations to form opinions on who is trustworthy in each situation

rather than blindly believing what is shared)
- Go against the grain (be willing to formulate a different opinion than the ones initially presented to you from previous professionals; be willing to shed light on an uncomfortable topic and confront ugly behaviors)

By mastering these skills, professionals will increase their ability and willingness to intervene in situations of psychological manipulation. Increasing the comfort level of professionals with recognition of the patterns of psychological manipulation and teaching awareness to transference/counter-transference issues that interfere with objective decision making are important competencies that can help prevent these abuses.

Implementation of education and training across systems is also integral to increasing resiliency in victims of chronic psychological abuse and preventing/stopping abuse from occurring. This education should cover a wide range of topics, including (but not limited to) the following: increased awareness and ability to recognize different forms of manipulation, more creative methods of providing safe interventions for victims of chronic psychological abuse, and heightened willingness for individuals "on the outside" to help victims take a stand against a form of abuse that is difficult to measure. Larger systems have the potential to effect wide ranging prevention and intervention policies and procedures that could greatly improve the success rate for victims of chronic psychological manipulation.

CHAPTER 12

Closure

Chronic psychological warfare is insidious, destructive, and devastating to its victims. Unchecked, it consumes everything, and everyone, in its path. The ability of individuals to recognize, and fight, an unseen enemy depends on their personality, awareness, perseverance, resilience, and protective factors. Without these factors in place, victims will fall prey to the destruction that accompanies this chronic form of abuse.

This book seeks to paint a very stark picture of these conditions, in order to increase alarm in all of us that this type of abuse is happening and needs to be addressed. Due to the very stealthy and sinister nature of this abuse, it often goes unnoticed and untreated. Every individual, whether they are a victim or unaffected in any way, must come together as a collective to fight against this type of treatment of others. While combating these situations feels uncomfortable and unpleasant, it is still necessary. Without the bravery and tenacity of countless victims, the outcomes of exposure to chronic psychological warfare would be very bleak indeed. It is the duty of every human to support these dogged individuals in their fight for survival.

When you pass through the waters, I will be with you; and through the rivers, they shall not overwhelm you; when you walk through fire you shall not be burned, and the flame shall not consume you. — Isaiah 43:2

Appendix A: Case Illustrations

Excerpts included below are fictional case illustrations presented for the purpose of further understanding the ways that chronic psychological abuse is manifested. Included in these is a breakdown of the patterns of psychological warfare utilized in each situation. These case illustrations are provided in order to validate victims for empowerment and to enhance awareness that they are not alone. There is power in sharing a story, specifically when dealing with a subject that many people find uncomfortable to address. Victims in these situations often experience high levels of fear and a belief that no one else is going through what they are experiencing. Additionally, there is a veil of secrecy surrounding psychological manipulation for victims; due to the unique nature of this type of abuse, it often does not help their cause to be open and upfront about what they are experiencing. Being able to see their encounters, or very similar ones on paper, can provide an enormous relief to victims as well as empower them. These case studies present a wide variety of backgrounds, both male and female, from diverse perspectives. The invasiveness of psychological warfare can impact anyone, without barriers, and there is no concrete method of measuring the damage it can do to its victims.

Case Illustration 1: Jeanine

Jeanine is in her early 50s. She was raised by a very traditional religious family of ranchers, who valued hard work and helping others. Jeanine was a "daddy's girl" and fondly remembers the special times she spent with her father, working on their farm or taking care of their horses. Growing up, she felt that she was always able to turn to her parents when needing help and believed that she would have a large family when she was an adult. Jeanine was closely involved in the church, along with her family, and often served as a volunteer to caretake children on Sundays. Jeanine did not have the finances to attend college but worked hard and was able to earn a scholarship for her first year. She left home, her first time away from it, and moved almost 1,500 miles to attend school. For the first time in her life, she felt lonely. She had no friends, no large family gatherings to look forward to, and no one to just sit with and talk to after a hard day. Jeanine found herself missing her family life more than she thought possible, and she often called home to share her homesickness. Her parents reminded her of the value of a college education and the need to focus on working hard in school instead of thinking about being homesick all the time. While Jeanine understood their perspective and valued their opinion, she just could not shake the feeling that she had made a mistake and would be wasting a year of her life stuck in a college dorm room miles away from her loved ones.

About 2 months after starting college, Jeanine found herself spending more and more time in the library on campus. It was quiet, she had always loved to read, and she was able to forget the isolating loneliness she felt when she sat in a peaceful corner of the library. She started taking her homework there and staying at the library every night until it closed. She dreaded heading back to her dorm room because she knew the feelings of seclusion that it would bring. One evening shortly before closing, a worker at the library happened to pass by her table and offered to put away the books she had not checked out.

Jeanine noticed right away that he was good looking, although he seemed quite a bit older than her. He was gracious and helpful, and she left without any further interactions with him. The next evening when she arrived at the library, she noticed him looking up from the welcome desk. He waved and smiled, then went back to working. Jeanine headed upstairs to the spot she typically sat at and commenced studying for an exam she had coming up. Before she knew it, most of the night had passed and she was exhausted. She stood up to leave, earlier than normal, and was surprised to see the worker come around the corner of the bookshelves. He stopped to visit briefly with her, on his way to file books, and introduced himself. He talked to Jeanine about some of the programs coming up at the library and recommended she go to some since it was obvious she enjoyed spending time there. Jeanine thanked him and they exchanged names.

Over the next week, Jeanine seemed to run into the worker, Randy, everywhere. She noticed that she started to look forward to seeing him because there was finally someone she knew and could visit with. He was always very affable and considerate of her, often checking into whether she needed anything on campus that he could help with. He was much older than her, by 15 years, and had worked on campus in various jobs for almost a decade. He told Jeanine in the course of their meetings that he was working on a novel and some different research topics for professors. She was fascinated at his writing topic (ways to cope with bereavement) and found herself inviting him to dinner. Shocked at her own forwardness, Jeanine almost cancelled at the last minute but felt that she deserved to enjoy her time at college. After all, she had worked so hard to be there and never took time away from her studies – even her own parents were encouraging her to do more with her free time.

The first date solidified Jeanine's feelings. She had never dated anyone seriously and immediately felt a connection to Randy that was unfamiliar to her. He told her he was engaged several years before, but his fiancé had wanted to move to a different area and they were not able to work it out. Jeanine understood his desire to stay close to home and admired that he had been true to this. It took only a few short weeks before the two of them were inseparable – he waited for her after classes, cooked dinner for her in his home, and she spent all of her free time with him. She stopped going to the library and he put in notice to work a job on campus that was more flexible with her schedule. Jeanine's parents expressed happiness that she was feeling a sense of belonging at college, although they wished to hear from her more. Jeanine even spent the holiday season close to campus with Randy, celebrating their first Christmas together. She noticed that for her first Christmas away from home she felt pretty good.

Jeanine loved that Randy went out of his way to compliment her. He seemed to admire her hard work and her intelligence so much, and he really listened to her ideas when she shared them. Randy believed in her and told her over and over she would make a difference someday. When Jeanine felt she would not do well on a test, Randy took time out of his schedule to quiz her and celebrated her successes with dinners out or dates in town. He always answered when she called and never stood her up. Jeanine never really questioned why he was so immediately available to her and never wondered why he did not have friends or family to spend time with – she was too happy that her loneliness was finally easing and there seemed to be a direction for her future.

Randy proposed to Jeanine shortly before her first year of college was over. She immediately said yes, even though he had not even met her parents yet. She was worried about being able to attend a second year; her scholarship would expire at the end of the first year and she had not heard back from financial aid yet. Randy solved it all by proposing and offering her an alternative – leave college to help him with his research. He felt like she was so brilliant and did not need to waste her time chasing a degree. Although in the back of her mind she wondered at her ability to put aside a goal she had worked so hard for, Jeanine also realized that in many ways this was the only viable solution that had come up. She no longer wanted to return home to live on the ranch with her parents. She wanted to start a family with Randy, and why wait when she knew exactly what her future should be?

Their wedding was fast and intimate – just the two of them. They waited until Jeanine's first year of college ended before she moved in with him, right after the wedding. Everything seemed wonderful – Randy and Jeanine planned to visit her parents' ranch that summer when he was on break. Four weeks before they were scheduled to leave, however, Jeanine found out she was pregnant. She was elated. She was so excited to tell her parents, and Randy had never seemed happier. They immediately started planning which room would be the nursery, talking about baby names, and immersing themselves in what they would need as parents. Jeanine did not tell her parents because she wanted to surprise them.

Less than 2 weeks after learning they were pregnant, Jeanine miscarried. Randy was at work when it happened and she called him in tears. He rushed home in a panic. When he found her and she explained what happened, instead of reassuring her and comforting her Randy was furious. Jeanine was in shock. He had never even been irritated, through their whole courtship. She did not recognize the yelling, swearing man standing over her and it scared her immensely. Jeanine's father had never been a fighter and was always easy going. She had no idea how to respond to Randy and started crying. He stormed out of the house and would not answer calls. That night, after Jeanine had gone to bed, he woke her up when he came into the room and turned on the light. She was exhausted from the miscarriage and from the emotions of the day, but Randy looked worse. His hair was a mess, his clothes were dirty, and his face was red and puffy. Her first thought was he had been drinking, but after she woke up a little, she was relieved this was not the case. Randy sat next to her on the bed and took her hands in his. He explained that he had spent the night driving, crying, and angry at God for the loss of the baby. He talked about his life dream of having a big family and his feelings of being a failure because he was not a father yet. Despite her own exhaustion and sadness, Jeanine felt awful for Randy. She understood his anger and disappointment, and part of her felt incredibly guilty that she had not been able to give him what he wanted more than anything. She vowed to forget his anger and focus on making a baby again – she knew once they were able to do that, everything would be wonderful.

The trip to meet her parents was not what Jeanine had expected it to be. They had no surprise to share, and both were still feeling down. Jeanine noticed that Randy was not as bubbly as normal, and although she understood, she was saddened that her parents were not seeing the real Randy. Although he was polite in all ways and spoke highly of their relationship to her parents, she could sense he had not recovered yet. One night after dinner, when they were alone, Randy mentioned off hand that he wondered why she had said she wanted a big family. He wondered if this was because her own family was small (she was the only child). He also asked her later if her parents had tried to have more children and been unable to, or just did not want more children. Jeanine had no answers for him and felt slightly worried that he was growing concerned she would not be able to have a big family. She brushed it off and marked it up to the stress they had both gone through.

Before they left, Jeanine's father pulled her aside and questioned if she was happy. She had not told her parents about the miscarriage – Randy's idea because he did not want her to feel like she had let them down in some way by not having the wonderful surprise she had planned. Jeanine wanted so badly to talk to her father about what happened, but with the precarious mood her husband had been in lately, she deferred. She smiled and said they were as happy as any couple could expect to be.

After their return home, the relationship changed for the worse. Randy grew more distant and rarely smiled. He started tracking Jeanine's periods and overly focused, in her mind, on whether they were pregnant. On one particularly bad night, Randy sat Jeanine down and pointed out some of the things he felt she was doing that were preventing them from having children. He had never expressed such negative feelings about her, and Jeanine felt embarrassed and ashamed. He even mentioned that she had gained weight since the miscarriage, which he felt was decreasing their odds of getting pregnant again. Jeanine was mute. This was not the Randy she knew so well. She no longer felt comfortable when he was home, and when he was gone, she found herself worrying about what mood he would come home in. To top it all off, her job helping Randy do research had fallen through. Now they had financial worries in addition to trying for a baby. Jeanine immediately started looking for work, but in a college town had difficulties finding a job after staying in college for only one year. Every potential employer wanted to know why she quit, and it always seemed like a deal breaker. With every turn down, Randy became more and more disappointed in her.

One morning after Jeanine had been sleepless because of worry about the upcoming house payment, Randy met her at the breakfast table and said he had been doing some thinking. He believed that her decision to quit college had placed their future in jeopardy because she was not employable. Jeanine was shocked that he thought this was her decision – she clearly remembered quitting college because he encouraged her to! She got angry and bit back at him, completely out of character for her. Randy's response was to laugh at her, which made her angrier. He pointed out that if it were not for his hard work, she would have no finances or place to live. Jeanine had had enough. She was incredulous that it had come to this, and she could no longer remember what it was like when they were carefree together. She told Randy she was leaving. He offered to help her pack.

Halfway through packing, Jeanine realized she had no vehicle that was not Randy's and nowhere to go. She had no money to stay in a hotel, as they had used up her savings weeks ago to pay the bills. She felt abandoned. How had it come to this? She remembered less than a year earlier being excited about traveling to meet her parents, and now she would have to call them to come pick her up. Jeanine was humiliated and blamed herself for the turn her marriage had taken. If she had been able to stay pregnant, if she had been more careful, if she had been able to find a job…too many ifs. She felt like she had completely messed up her chance at happiness.

Contrite and ashamed, Jeanine found herself begging Randy to let her stay. She did not feel like she could demean herself by telling her parents the truth. Randy was very hesitant and said he felt like their marriage was over. Jeanine promised him she would make changes, and that he was the most important person in the world to her. She vowed to lose weight, take care of herself, and find a job no matter what. Randy eventually came around and said he would give her another chance.

This pattern happened for years. Jeanine was never able to get pregnant, although she did bounce from job to job. With some experience under her belt, it became easier to get a job but always difficult to keep one. Randy always seemed to push her to get promoted almost immediately, and the pressure would end up being too much. Jeanine left most jobs to start over somewhere that they felt would give her more opportunity. Despite her best efforts, she continued to slip further into depression and blamed herself for the mess that was her marriage. The longer it went on, the more she avoided telling her parents the truth. They stopped going home for holidays and she rarely answered their calls. Jeanine was miserable and alone.

It took the death of her mother to bring Jeanine home. She had no choice, and by that time her relationship with Randy was bad enough he refused to go with her. Jeanine took one suitcase and walked out. She broke down under the stress of the loss and poured out what had happened to her father. He immediately refused to allow her to return to Randy and made arrangements for her belongings to be brought home. Randy filed for divorce. Jeanine spent many years learning to rebuild her self-confidence and trust others. She constantly felt like people were judging her and was hypersensitive to anyone being upset with her. Eventually, with the support of her father and a lot of very challenging personal work, Jeanine was able to find a job she loved and started dating a man from a nearby town. She never had children but felt that if she had, they would have reminded her too much of her earlier failures. She characterized herself as "sort of happy most of the time" and felt like this was a huge victory for her in her later years.

Patterns of psychological manipulation identified:

- Grooming behaviors – early in the relationship, Randy carefully observed Jeanine's habits and made sure he was always present. He was helpful, assisting her first with minor things like putting her books away and later with problem solving financial crises like losing her scholarship. He listened intently to her, tried to anticipate her needs, and built her up with praise.
- Unrealistic expectations of relationships – Randy built Jeanine up to be perfect in his mind, which worked for them until she miscarried and crashed his idea of perfection. This catalyst also destroyed his feelings for Jeanine eventually because she did not live up to his expectation of perfection.
- Lack of empathy – Randy was unable to understand the emotions behind Jeanine's miscarriage and infertility. He viewed this only

through a lens of his own emotions. He was not able to understand her employment issues and what she was going through when attempting to find a job; instead, he used this as ammunition to blame her for what he was not "getting."

- Deferred accountability – Randy did not take accountability for his part in any of their issues and blamed Jeanine for the problems arising in their marriage, finances, etc.
- Gaslighting – Randy made up blatant lies when Jeanine was vulnerable, which she went along with. She also started to question herself on her memories of what had really been said (such as his desire for her to quit work, then anger at her later for quitting).
- Restricted emotions – Randy alternated between elated and angry. Jeanine never noticed other emotions, and they never discussed his feelings about most topics. He went from happy all of the time during courtship to enraged when she could not give him what he

wanted in marriage. Once he got to this point, he no longer exhibited positive emotions.

Case Illustration 2: Tom

Tom was a mama's boy from birth. His father passed away while his mother was pregnant, and she carried him everywhere with her after he was born – they did not leave each other's side until he started school. He fondly remembers those years as "golden" because he felt nothing could separate him from his mother.

In 3rd grade, Tom's mother remarried. His stepfather, Barry, was actually one of his teachers at the elementary school. He took him to baseball games on the weekends and taught him to cook. While Tom missed the time that he had his mother's full attention, he was not angry about Barry coming into their lives. He knew his mother worried less about money with Barry's job.

Through the first year of marriage, Barry was very attentive to Tom. He noticed when he was upset at home and at school, and he was always ready to listen. Tom preferred to talk to his mother, but Barry insisted he needed to get to know Tom on a deeper level because he loved him and wanted him to feel safe. Tom eventually grew used to Barry being everywhere he and his mother were. At the start of 4th grade, Tom's mother lost her job, putting financial strain on the family. Barry started to lecture Tom about taking care of his mother, and Tom remembers Barry trying to teach him about ways young kids could make money. Barry reminded Tom that if he was not in the house, Tom would not be able to take care of his mother.

One lunch time at school, Barry sat with Tom while they ate. He told Tom he was worried about his mother – she had been really sad that morning and seemed to not be herself. This worried Tom; he loved his mother so much and wanted her to be happy. He was distracted during school and did not pay attention in class. When he got home, his mother seemed fine. He asked her why she had been upset that morning and she blew it off, saying she had never felt better.

After that day, worries crept into Tom's mind more often. Was his mother hiding something from him? Was she ok? Was he doing something wrong to upset her, and she didn't want to tell him? He got more and more distracted in school with these worries, and eventually a parent teacher conference was called to discuss his performance dropping. After the meeting, Tom's mom cried. She said she did not understand why he wasn't trying, and she was upset that he had not come to her to talk about it. Barry said he wished Tom had brought it up; he mentioned that he is at the same school every day and had no idea Tom was struggling. Barry wanted to know why Tom had not asked him for help. Tom wasn't sure how to say what he was feeling and didn't say anything.

The next morning before school, Barry pulled Tom aside to tell him he needed to make a better effort at school. He said his mother was too disappointed in him to bring it up and that Tom's behaviors at school were making her feel horrible. Barry said Tom needed to keep his mother happy and encouraged him to come to Barry with any problems. Barry said it would only make Tom's mother worry more about him if he were to bring them up to her.

The thought of hurting his mother scared Tom. His mother was the most important person in the world to him. He promised himself to do better in school so she would not worry about him, but everywhere he went it seemed like Barry was there –

reminding him to try harder and telling him constantly he needed to take care of his mother. Barry took every opportunity to tell Tom all of the reasons he was not enough and how his failures would eventually ruin his mother if he did not correct them. The pressure was overwhelming for Tom. He felt like he could never make good enough decisions and he started to dread talking to Barry. He tried avoiding him at school, and by the end of 6th grade Tom was relieved that he would finally have freedom at a different school.

7th grade didn't turn out like Tom expected. The pressure at home from Barry was immense compared to the previous year. Without seeing him every day at school, Barry was even more aggressive with Tom at home. He constantly harped on him to do more chores, get straight As, dress better, and speak more politely. Tom felt like he could do nothing right. He wanted so much to talk to his mother about his feelings, but his fear of disappointing her and creating even more problems was too much. Tom started making stupid decisions at school with his friends, like ditching class and smoking weed. He started to get angry at Barry and argued with him at home. He started getting edgy with his mother, who he had always been close to, and felt like she was siding with Barry over him. One night he heard his parents talking and was incensed to hear Barry telling his mother that he wished Tom would just open up more and share what was really going on. Tom also overheard Barry comforting his mother and sharing his sadness that Tom would not talk to his mother like he used to. Tom's mother said he was not the same boy he used to be.

Tom felt betrayed and that it was them against him. His acting out increased through junior high, and by 10th grade he had been involved in the legal system and was sent away from home. His anger fueled his behaviors throughout his teenage years, driving him further and further from his mother and Barry. He had relapse after relapse even into young adulthood and was in and out of jail. By his mid-20s, Tom refused to go near his family and could not stand the sight of Barry. His mother was heartbroken but felt like her marriage was her responsibility; she reasoned that Tom was a grown man and needed her even less now.

Tom's mother died of cancer when he was 32. He never reconnected with her before her death, and every day he feels guilt and grief at this. Tom has refused contact with Barry since his mother passed away and has spent years in and out of rehab dealing with his addictions. He has recognized the wedges that were driven between him and his mother by Barry, but he continues to feel that he could have done something different and made more of an effort. Tom feels much of his addiction has been a way to numb himself to his constant feelings of shame and guilt. Barry is almost retired as a teacher and has become involved as a volunteer in a local community group for parents whose children became involved with the legal system. He often gives guest lectures about his experience in this area and offers to informally counsel parents who are going through the same issues.

Patterns of psychological manipulation identified:
- Grooming behaviors – Barry groomed Tom early in their relationship to gain his trust. He paid special attention to him and made sure to express how much he cared for him. This ended once he gained Tom's trust.
- Manipulation – Barry manipulated Tom's trust to drive wedges

between him and his mother, for the sake of isolating Tom.
- Excessive guilt and fear – Barry used the guilt Tom felt over his behaviors against him and as a catalyst for more control. He also instilled excessive fear in Tom about the family's future.
- Emotional control - Barry used Tom's strong emotions about his mother as an area of vulnerability, to attack him repeatedly until he was successful at breaking him.
- Intellectual Bullying – Barry was careful to present himself as an expert and used his abuse of Tom to further sponsor his role as an authority.

Case Illustration 3: Malia

Malia is the youngest of 5 siblings, all boys. Her parents divorced when she was very young, and she does not remember them being together. Her father is a workaholic and does not see Malia as much as she would like. She is close to her mother. At age 25, she became one of the first female attorneys in her community to be offered a position at a federal level. She is ruthless in the court room, extremely intelligent, and beautiful.

Malia has been married to Wade since she was 19. They met in college and married immediately. Although her parents were hesitant due to her age, they fully supported (and paid for) her wedding. They have no children because neither wants children to interfere with their careers. Wade is an architect and designs commercial buildings. They both work long hours during the week and play hard on the weekends with their friends. On the surface, they appear to have it all – growing bank accounts, youth, and flashy jobs.

Behind closed doors, Malia attends therapy every week because of the tremendous anxiety she experiences. She has a constant feeling of doom and is paranoid about what her colleagues think of her. She feels that every misstep she makes in the court room will come back to haunt her years down the road, and she has developed an ulcer due to the stress. She also shares openly with her therapist, whom she has been seeing for over 2 years, about her marriage. She has shared Wade's anger and resentment toward her – for having both parents around still (his passed away in a car accident when he was

15), for making more money than him, and for being so well liked by others. Malia recounts that she left Wade for a period of 6 months 2 years ago and had an affair during that time. She identifies that Wade has never forgiven her for this and continues to be intensely angry at her. At times, Malia wishes she had filed for divorce – but as an attorney she knows the process can be excruciating and can't imagine the embarrassment to her professionally and personally if she were to do this. She lives with fears that Wade will expose her affair to others, as he did to her mother during a family vacation. Malia has started sleeping with a knife in her bed lately – during a heated argument recently, Wade pushed her down the stairs. It was the only time he has ever been physical with her and it centered around her staying late for dinner with a male colleague to celebrate a victory in the firm. Malia feels guilty about this incident and believes that her past indiscretion warrants Wade's distrust in her current relationship, although she has no romantic feelings toward her colleague.

Much of Malia's therapy centers around her extreme guilt and anxiety over her marriage. She fears what would happen if she were to walk away, and she is struggling to keep it together at work. Her physical health is suffering, and she has lost weight. On the weekends, Malia and Wade continue to go out with friends and he is always loving and attentive when with them. Their acquaintances and friends continue to believe they have "the perfect marriage." Behind closed doors, Wade alternates between silent and sullen or angry. Malia identifies they no longer have sex or show physical affection if they are alone. Her parents and brothers have no idea what life is like at home, as they all enjoy Wade and get along well with him. Wade and her brothers hunt together every year and anytime the family gets together he is the life of the party. Malia knows the blow to her family that would happen if she were to leave Wade.

Malia has started having thoughts about getting pregnant but pushes this to the back burner until she is promoted in her career. She rationalizes that by that time, Wade will be making more money as a senior architect, which she believes would lessen his anger at her earnings. She states that although she feels extreme anxiety, her life with Wade in many ways is more comfortable and easier than it would be elsewhere. She has a beautiful home, a family who gets along well with her husband, friends, and makes loads of money. Malia acknowledges that her view of the future is not what she thought it would be when she was younger, but she believes this is the best she can hope for given her circumstances.

Patterns of psychological manipulation identified:
- Emotional control – Wade uses his emotions to control Malia. He focuses on her past indiscretion to control her behaviors and uses guilt to manipulate her.
- Excessive guilt and fear – Wade tries to make Malia feel excessively guilty over things, from her affair to the amount of money she earns.
- Victim stance – Wade has adopted the victim stance due to the imbalance in their careers/popularity with others and Malia's past affair. He takes no accountability in his unhappiness and places blame on her shoulders for his emotions.
- Distrustful – Wade mistrusts Malia's intentions and relationships, including benign and

harmless ones. He punishes her based on this mistrust.
- Insecure – Wade is insecure about who he is as a person and his success in life. He tries to cover this up with punishing Malia for her personal strengths and is excessively jealous of her accomplishments.

Case Illustration 4: Ben

Ben was 12 when he first went to foster care. Both of his parents were arrested simultaneously, for drug related charges. He was split from his 7 siblings and placed in a foster care home on the other side of town. Ben was the oldest sibling in his family, and he felt responsible for not being there to take care of his brothers and sisters. He attended a different school than them and found this even more challenging. After his parents were released from jail, Ben and several of the older siblings were placed back in their care. The reunification was short-lived. Within 4 months, Ben's father was arrested again, and his mother deemed to be neglecting her children. Ben was placed outside of the home, and this time he did not return.

Through adolescence, Ben moved from family to family. He vividly recalls a 16 month stay in a foster home (his last placement) where he was the only child in the home. He remembers his foster "father" in this home, who he describes as "dangerously charming." Ben identifies that his foster father was a well-known community business owner and offered to take him in to demonstrate to others his care and concern for the children impacted by parental decisions in their town. Ben's foster father served on a community initiative panel that focused on reducing instances of childhood abandonment and neglect.

Ben characterizes two separate people when talking about his foster father. He describes his public persona, of a delightful man and persuasive speaker – who was on fire for youth causes. Privately, he remembers the chilling interactions in which his foster father would berate him for not behaving appropriately in public. Ben reminisces about the constant anger he felt emanating from his foster father behind closed doors, and he describes several incidents in which he feared for his physical safety. He acknowledges that his foster father never physically abused him, but Ben remembers being scared of this often throughout the time he lived in the home. He also recounts staying up late at night, listening for the footsteps outside his door. He remembers his sweating and panicked breathing while he wondered what his foster father was doing or when he would come in. Ben denies that his foster father ever entered his room but vividly recalls the terror he felt internally at the game being played during his nights there.

As Ben aged out of foster care, he felt a profound sense of relief and freedom. He went on to serve in the military, far from his hometown. He never returned. Ben has had challenges romantically and seems to always choose the "wrong" relationships. He identifies a string of women for whom he had never measured up, and he could not seem to make the changes they needed in order to stay. Ben's most recent relationship, a short-lived marriage, ended following an extramarital affair he had with a coworker. Ben regrets his relationship failures but also feels a level of comfort that he has not had children – he has deep rooted fears that he would be a bad father. Instead of taking the chance to find out, Ben tends to avoid situations that could lead to having kids. He is proud of his military service and feels that he has done well for himself. He is able to support himself financially and is starting a home construction company since his discharge from the service. Although he wishes at times for a companion, he believes that the best choice for his future is to focus on his career and not on building a family.

Patterns of psychological manipulation identified:

- Intellectual bullying – Ben's foster father presented himself as an expert on issues related to raising foster children, but behind closed doors he bullied Ben.
- Emotional control – Ben's foster father used Ben's emotions to exert power and control over him. He consistently focused on his faults in order to prove he was unworthy, and he played cat-and-mouse games designed to show Ben who had the power in the relationship.
- Excessive guilt and fear –Ben's foster father used fear as a weapon to intimidate him and control his behaviors.

Case Illustration 5: Louise

Louise lives alone, in a small flat that she can afford on her disability and retirement income. Sometimes she thinks about the different boyfriends who came and went in her later years and wonders whether it would have been a better decision to settle down again. She doubts it, although she likes to remember some of the enjoyable times they had together. Louise has noticed as she ages that the enjoyable times are easier to remember, although the times she recalls as dangerous still crop up every now and then. She does feel like the occurrence of these memories has lessened over the years, which she is grateful for in addition to being relieved. Sometimes, when she recalls particularly awful times, she is unsure how she successfully made it to the age she is now.

Louise married Gerald when they were 16. They had no choice but to get married – she was pregnant and her only parent had just died in a work related accident. Gerald promised to take care of her, and their baby, and that was that. For about 6 months it seemed like they were going to make it ok. Louise remembers they had no money, but Gerald worked hard and they were able to eat and keep their home. Once the baby was born, things turned bad. Gerald started working extra hours to try to make more money and came home exhausted, angry, and mean. He blamed Louise and the baby for his hard hours at a job he hated. He talked constantly about the damage he was doing to his body by working such long hours, and he could never understand why he was doing it. Gerald felt like Louise and the baby were a drain on him and his future. There were several nights that Gerald kept Louise up, with the baby crying for hours in the next room, and made her pay him back for his hard work by doing whatever he wanted sexually. When she begged to stop and go take care of the baby, Gerald would hold her down and punish her. In the morning, he never failed to remind her before he left for work that if she had just taken care of his needs, like he was taking care of hers, they all would have had a more peaceful night. After a while, Louise started to believe him. She did learn that doing what he asked made the least amount of trouble for them all, and more than anything she wanted to keep the baby safe.

After the baby turned 2, Gerald came home less. Louise was glad but knew that when he did come home there would be hell to pay. She was sure he had started up a relationship with Tilde on the street over from their home, but she never dared to ask him. People talked at church, and Gerald and Tilde seemed to sit next to each other a lot those days. Louise actually liked that he started up with Tilde because it took him out of her hair several nights a week. She hoped Tilde would keep him busy and get the short end of the stick so she could sleep in peace.

Gerald continued to spend 1 or 2 nights a week with Louise for years. He refused to let her get a divorce, even though she worked up the courage to ask him. He reminded her that without his financial support she would have nowhere to live. He refused to take care of her or the little one if she left him. Louise tried to bring up Tilde, to explain to Gerald that she would be happy for them and let them live together in peace, but this just made Gerald angrier. He told her he was working nights and became livid at her suggestion that he would lower himself to having an affair. Gerald told Louise he was shocked at her low morals and berated her for thinking such horrible thoughts about him. He even asked her what their pastor would think if he brought up her suggestion to him – and wondered out loud if she was fit to be raising their daughter with ideas like that. Louise begged him not to say anything.

Louise eventually stopped going to church because she could not keep from feeling ashamed and worried when she was there. She constantly looked over her shoulder whenever she left the house with her child and experienced worry thoughts all the time about who might be watching her and judging her as a parent. When Gerald stopped coming home any nights, he also stopped paying her bills at the house. Louise was forced to get a job to survive. While she was gone from her child, she felt scared and worried that Gerald would do something at the school, before she could get there to pick him up. When she was home, she was scared that at any moment Gerald would orchestrate it so she would lose him. Louise felt like she was losing her mind and was not sure how much more she could take.

When their son turned 10, Louise got a late night visitor from the sheriff's office. Her panic turned to relief when she was told that Gerald had died in a vehicle accident on his way home from work. Louise was shocked at just how relieved she felt, and at the freedom she experienced after Gerald's death. It took a few months before she felt comfortable going back out into the community, and she ended up finding a new church. Her son did well in school and eventually graduated high school and moved away to start a family of his own. Louise often remembers that although she was physically free, it took many years for her to stop looking over her shoulder and worrying about "what was coming." She recounts this time as an awakening of sorts and feels like she learned who she really was during these years.

In her later years, Louise feels like she accomplished a lot. She held down a job at a local newspaper for years and eventually became an editor. She was able to retire to the city her son lives in and purchase her flat. She has had trouble with her memory as she ages and has gone blind because of untreated cataracts. Overall, Louise feels like she was finally able to escape Gerald and is working on letting the memories go now. She often wonders at the power they still hold over her, decades after they happened, and believes those years in her life have negatively affected her memory as she aged.

Patterns of psychological manipulation identified:

- Victim stance – Gerald consistently used the victim stance with Louise. He blamed his type of work and his misfortunes on her. He felt like she needed to caretake his needs because of his unjustified misfortunes, attributed to Louise and the baby. Gerald held Louise responsible for the path his life took and did not take accountability himself.
- Sexual control – Gerald used sexual interactions as a method to control and exert dominance over Louise. He manipulated her into doing what he wanted sexually as revenge for his unhappiness.
- Gaslighting – Gerald used blatant dishonesty in regards to his affair. Although it was fairly common knowledge that he was having an affair, his gaslighting techniques worked with Louise and she felt convinced that he was really just working long hours. He started out with smaller scale lies and graduated to bigger lies as he saw it worked. Louise was living in a reality that most people would be

shocked at, but because of the gaslighting techniques Gerald used she rarely questioned it.
- Financial control – Gerald used his status as financial supporter to control Louise's emotions, thoughts, and behaviors. He threatened her, and their child's, future through the use of financial control.
- Creation of paranoia – Gerald used threats and suggestions of impending doom to create paranoia for Louise regarding her parenting and the security of their child. These tactics were successful enough that Louise stopped utilizing her support system at her church due to the paranoia she was experiencing.

References

1. Beck, J.S. *Cognitive behavior therapy: Basics and beyond*. 2nd ed., New York, NY, US: Guilford Press. 2011.
2. Blaufarb, Rafe. *Napoleon: What Made Him Great?* https://www.historynet.com/napoleon-made-great.htm, Military History, 2012.
3. Brown, A.D., Ph.D. *Protective factors and risk factors associated with trauma, the process of recovery and resiliency*. 2017.
4. Cassidy, R. Michael. *Sharing Shared Secrets: Is It (Past) Time for a Dangerous Person Exception to the Clergy Penitent Privilege*. 44 Wm. & Mary L. Rev. 1627, 1638, 2003.
5. Center for Substance Abuse Treatment (US). *Trauma-Informed Care in Behavioral Health Services*. Rockville (MD): Substance Abuse and Mental Health Services Administration (US), 2014. (Treatment Improvement Protocol (TIP) Series, No. 57.) Chapter 3, Understanding the Impact of Trauma. Available from:

https://www.ncbi.nlm.nih.gov/books/NBK207191/.
6. Chan, Amy. *Genghis Khan's Secrets of Success.* Military History, 2007.
7. Crocq, Marc-Antoine. *Milestones in the history of personality disorders.* Dialogues in Clinical Neuroscience v 15 (2), 2013.
8. *Diagnostic and statistical manual of mental disorders*, 5th ed., American Psychiatric Association, 2013.
9. Dutton, K. *The Wisdom of Psychopaths: What Saints, Spies, and Serial Killers Can Teach Us About Success.* 2012.
10. Freud, Sigmund. *The Dynamics of Transference.* The Standard Edition of the Complete Psychological Works of Sigmund Freud, Volume XII, 1911-1913.
11. Gordon, Robert M. *Transference and Counter-Transference: A Psychoanalytic Perspective on the Attorney-Client Relationship.* nassaubar.org/articles/transference-and-countertransference-a-psychoanalytic-perspective-on-the-attorney-client-relationship/.
12. Hamilton, Patrick. *Gaslight.* 1938.
13. Hermann, Henry R. *Alternate Human Behavior.* Dominance and Aggression in Humans and Other Animals, 2017.

14. https://justice.gov/ovw/domestic-violence
15. https://www.apa.org/ptsd-guideline/patients-and-families/cognitive-behavioral.
16. Journal Psyche. *Revisiting Carl Rogers Theory of Personality.* http://journalpsyche.org/revisiting-carl-rogers-theory-of-personality (2015).
17. Macias, Amanda. *A fully-fledged masochist: Inside the CIA's psychological profile of Adolf Hitler.* https://www.thejournal.ie/hitler-psychological-profile-2620137-Feb2016/ , 2016.
18. Mecke, V. *A Reference for Psychodynamic Theories.* Review of the book Psychodynamic Theory for Clinicians. D. Bienenfeld, PsycCRITIQUES, 51(41) 2006.
19. Motzkin, J., Newman, J., Kiehl, K., and Koenigs, M. *Reduced Prefrontal Connectivity in Psychopathy.* Journal of Neuroscience. 31 (48) 2011.
20. Nagler, Ursa K.J., Reiter, Katharina J., Furtner, Marco R., and Rauthmann, John F. *Is there a 'dark intelligence'? Emotional intelligence is used by dark personalities to*

emotionally manipulate others. Personality and Individual Differences, 2014.
21. National Institute of Justice. *Interventions for Domestic Violence Offenders: Cognitive Behavioral Therapy.* https://www.crimesolutions.gov/PracticeDetails.aspx?ID=16
22. New World Encyclopedia. *Psychological Warfare.* https://www.newworldencyclopedia.org/entry/Psychological_warfare.
23. Radel, F. Robert, and Labbe, Andrew A. *The Clergy-Penitent Privilege: An Overview.* 2015.
24. Rayfield, Donald. *Stalin and His Hangmen: The Tyrant and Those Who Killed for Him.* Random House Publishing Group, 229, 2007.
25. Redmond L. W. *Spiritual coping tools of religious victims of childhood sexual abuse.* J Pastoral Counsel, 68 (1-2): 3, 2014.
26. Rees, Laurence. *Stalin the Puppetmaster.* https://www.historynet.com/stalin-the-puppetmaster.htm.
27. Reisman, Miriam. *PTSD Treatment for Veterans: What's Working, What's New, and What's Next. P&T,* 2016.
28. Scanlon, Mike. *History: Napoleon was a master manipulator Philip Dwyer's book*

Citizen Emperor reveals. Newcastle Herald, 2014.
29. United Nations General Assembly. *The Universal Declaration of Human Rights.* General Assembly Resolution 217A, 1948.
30. Zamoyski, Adam. *The Personality Traits that Led to Napoleon Bonaparte's Epic Downfall.* https://www.history.com/news/napoleon-bonaparte-downfall-reasons-personality-traits, 2019.

www.ingramcontent.com/pod-product-compliance
Lightning Source LLC
Chambersburg PA
CBHW070552010526
44118CB00012B/1295